ONCE A BRAT...

Marilyn Celeste Morris

AmErica House
Baltimore

First printing

ISBN: 1-59129-252-2
PUBLISHED BY AMERICA HOUSE BOOK PUBLISHERS
www.publishamerica.com
Baltimore

Printed in the United States of America

Dedication:

To the memory of my father, RM Morris, Major, USA
01168836 for making me a Military Brat

To my mother, Frances Garrett Morris,
for helping me live through it

To all Military Brats everywhere

MILITARY-BRATS REGISTRY
WWW.MILITARY-BRATS.COM
466 ORANGE ST, #280
REDLANDS, CA 92374

Acknowledgements:

To Dr. Tom Drysdale, for being the catalyst for The American Overseas Schools Historical Society, where Military Brats can house their "sacred relics."

And for suggesting that I, as one of the dwindling reserves of "older Brats" record my life as a Military Brat from 1938 to 1958. Thank you for your support and encouragement along the way.

The City of Wichita KS, for giving Military Brats a home.

Marc Curtis, for the Military Brats Registry—Thank you, Marc, for helping thousands of Brats find each other.

Joe Condrill, founder of Overseas Brats, for hosting regional and national conventions.

DoDDs Educators, for being in our lives wherever we were.

And for the members of the newsgroup alt.culture military-brats, some of whom I have met face-to-face, some I have yet to meet, but we are all nevertheless members of the same extended family.

Foreword

BRAT: def.: (1) An unruly child
def: (2) A child of the military

We wear the "Brat" name with pride; those who argue that the term is demeaning simply don't understand.

Once a Brat is not intended to be a serious study of children of the military.

It is neither an apology nor a rallying cry for our unique experiences.

While some of my fellow Military Brats, missionary kids, children of the diplomatic corps, oil company employees' offspring and others may find similarities in my narrative, I must emphasize that this book is based solely on events transpiring between 1938 and 1958, with comments on how the Military Brat experience affected my life.

My mother made the dreaded phone call early on a Thursday.

"Your dad died this morning at six o'clock."

I took it for granted that my father would be buried in Fort Sam Houston's cemetery. I also assumed he would be buried in his uniform, so I was somewhat surprised that Mother had not laid out his dress blues, but a dark suit—a "civilian" suit.

"Mom," I protested. "Don't you think Dad should be buried in his uniform?"

"No," she answered slowly as if she were talking to a child. "Remember, your father had been retired much longer than he was in the Army."

That was a shock almost worse than the news of my father's death. A civilian longer than a U.S. Army officer? Well, I thought, that may be the truth, as my mother and father knew it, and to a large extent, the truth for my two younger brothers. But for *my* entire childhood, from 1938 until my second year of college in 1958, the truth was my father lived and breathed the US Military. Therefore, every moment of my first twenty years of life was dictated by the whims of the United States Army. Where I would live. Where I would go to school. What friends I would accumulate. What discipline I would attain, and what goals I would aspire to. From the sound of Reveille each morning to Retreat each evening, I was reminded of my station in life: I was a Military Brat.

I was always "different." I was always the new kid in the classroom, the new kid on the block if we lived as "civilians" in town, the new kid in one of the cookie-cutter quarters in an endless series of military compounds.

I still choke up when the National Anthem is played, whether at a ballpark or concert. The strains of Sousa marches bring tears as I picture parades of uniformed men saluting as the flag passes. "Yes, Sir" and "No, Sir" have not yet ceased to be an automatic part of my vocabulary. Merely climbing into a cab on a dark night in Chicago, the smell of fermented cabbage assaulting my nostrils caused me to blurt to the driver, "You're from Korea, aren't you?"

I saw the reflection of his white teeth in the rear-view mirror as he grinned, "Yah. How you know that?"

My one word reply: "Kim Chi."

The yearning to hear the Austrian/Bavarian phrase *"Gruss Gott"* bestowed on me whether entering or leaving a shop or merely passing a native on the streets along the Danube River will never leave me.

I will always cry at *Taps*, not so much as it reminds me of my father's military funeral, but that it reminds me of my own lost childhood. *Taps* may as well have been sounded for *me* at my father's retirement ceremony for a unique part of me died, too: That part of me that reveled in being an officer's daughter with certain privileges of rank along with that part of me that rebelled—in spirit at least—against the restrictions imposed upon me by that same privilege of rank: officer's kids must not misbehave under any circumstance as it reflects on your father's career. Military Brats were as regimented as our fathers.

I cried in recognition when I read Pat Conroy's foreword to Mary Edwards Wertsch's landmark study, *Military Brats: Legacies of Childhood from Inside the Fortress.* Like many other Brats, I have the uncanny ability to close a door and never look back. When I lost my house to a divorce some years ago, I felt strangely distant, uncaring, that the house was no longer mine. I shut the door and turned the lock, got into my car and drove away. Without a tear. Never going back.

I can do the same with a job. Although I made friends easily in my jobs as a temporary secretary, when the time came for my departure (orders), I gathered my few personal objects, bid my co-workers farewell, and walked out the door. A day or two later, I was in another place, with other people, and I had no time to mourn the prior loss.

Marriage suffered as well. When I'm gone, I'm gone. No lingering goodbyes, regrets, longings for what could have been. It was over.

I will never know what it's like to live in one town, in one house, for longer than a few years. I longed for that, some time ago, but now I wonder if the life I lived—a global nomad in a sense—wasn't the best kind of life for me. I gained an enormous appreciation for my country, my flag and all things patriotic.

I was somewhat bemused by the surge of patriotism displayed after 9-11-01. I confided to my Brat friends, "I don't know what all the fuss is all about. After all, we were raised with all this." I had long ago placed the "Proud to be a Military Brat" sticker on my car and wore my pin just as proudly. Some people snickered at the word "Brat" on my lapel pin while others flew to my pin as a moth to a flame. They understood. They were Military Brats.

In civilian schools, I was way ahead of others with the exception of math, which I understand is a common deficiency in many Military Brats. We were all studying fractions when our new school taught decimals. And vice versa. History, languages and geography were a snap, however. I gaped in astonishment when a high school student confused *Austria* with *Australia* and asked if I had a kangaroo.

Poor souls—having to live their entire lives in Killeen, Texas. They didn't know the ecstasy of Bavaria in the summertime; concerts in the town square, the terror of knowing the enemy was right across the Danube River, or the 38th Parallel, and could attack at any given moment—and they did in the case of South Korea.

We were in Paris on June 25, 1950. At the news, we hurried back to Dad's base in Austria, our hearts thudding in fear that war would simultaneously erupt in Europe.

While we were in Korea two years earlier, we had experienced problems with the Russians. They had control of our electricity above the 38th parallel. Now and then, as we watched a movie in a tent theatre, the power suddenly went off. But we didn't miss a beat—generators were cranked up, and the movie continued.

Homework was completed by kerosene lantern—no electricity was no excuse for not handing in our assignments. Not in a dependents' school, no sir.

In Europe, we were obliged to keep a suitcase packed and under the bed, ready to evacuate and meet at pre-determined checkpoints, just in case.

Pro-Communist May Day parades gave our teachers near heart attacks when we hung out our schoolroom windows and taunted the marchers for their squeaky shoes; we could hear them coming from blocks away. On those May Days, we rode home in an army bus with armed guards "riding shotgun" hearing stones pound the sides of the bus—only to hear a rumor that those weren't stones but bullets.

I doubt that was accurate, and I'll probably never know. Personally, I found the possibility of being involved in an "international incident" both exciting and historic. Never concerned for my safety, I knew the Powers that Be would take good care of us Dependents.

Years after we had left Seoul, Korea, my father, who had returned after the Korean War to serve as Military Advisor to the ROK, sent pictures of our former quarters. Aerial strafing and bombings had pockmarked HQG27. All the windows were boarded up, and South Korean soldiers were scavenging the hardwood floors for firewood. I looked at my bedroom window thinking, *I played with my homemade dollhouse right there.*

I recall my father sweating the exquisite timing required for our drive from Linz to Vienna through the Russian Zone of Occupation, lest we be arrested for "spying." It was difficult to keep my face expressionless as Russian guards peered intently at our "papers"—holding them upside down.

As I sat under a huge tree near the Spanish Guard Tower on Donatusgasse, in Linz, Austria, looking over the Danube River into the Russian Zone of Occupation, I realized that if I could see them, they could see me. Immediately upon arrival, my dad drilled into my head, *"Don't ever cross the bridge into the Russian Zone."*

Our fear, then, was of the Russians. We managed to co-exist.

I was to recall the edict: *"Never cross the bridge over the Danube"* years later when on a nostalgic return to Linz with my grown daughter, Terri, we took a wrong turn and *actually crossed the Danube.*

My reaction was knee-jerk, instantaneous, and highly vocal.

"We can't cross the river," I gasped. My daughter and our friend Jennifer looked at me, startled. *"I mean, we couldn't do that when I lived here..."*

Realizing how insane that must have sounded, my voice trailed off.

But I remained uneasy until Jennifer turned the jeep around, and we departed the Forbidden Russian Zone.

For the remainder of the afternoon, lest I should suffer another trauma, we were careful not to drive over any bridge spanning the Beautiful Blue Danube.

Once a Brat, always a Brat.

As one of the "older" Brats who paved the way for those who followed, I consider myself one of the fortunate few who will always remain, at the core of her being, a Military Brat.

Friendships

I always made friends the very first day, wherever we went. I always affiliated myself with the "in" crowd, the leaders. How I managed to pick the best and brightest students as friends, I don't know. Why weren't some of them NOT leaders, popular, and "good" kids? It must have been some kind of "Brat Radar." My best friend in Austria was the general's daughter. Janie Elmore was with me when my dad called from the hospital and told me that my mom had had another boy. Janie cried with me in disappointment. I had wanted a baby sister.

Being the a friend of the general's daughter certainly had its perks. First run movies were shown in their magnificent quarters nearly every night. I was offered, and accepted, a bit of wine with the movie. The general's quarters also had a swimming pool, and I remember one incident where we kids ganged up on the butler and tossed him into the water. We didn't figure he would tell on us, and he must not have, because we never did get in trouble over that.

One night during a slumber party, we got into the liquor

cabinet and drank a little hard liquor. None of us really got drunk, but we acted as if we were. And we all had horrible headaches the next morning, so I suppose that was punishment enough and we never did it again.

When it came time to move, friendships became more of a burden, and I had to "unhook." One of the ways in which I unhooked was to pick a fight before he/she/I left. It made parting easier. I was mad at him/her anyway. *My inability to sustain long-term relationships handicapped my adult relationships. I lacked the skills in apologizing, making up, overlooking faults. I had never bothered with repairing or sustaining relationships; why bother, when one of us would soon be gone? I could simmer and sulk with the best of 'em, but never had the need to resolve any differences that arose between friends.*

Rank:

The thing about being an officer's kid was that I was never allowed to associate with children of lower-ranking personnel. Sons and daughters of enlisted personnel were off limits to me. When Dad found out my friend Ada Castaldi's father was enlisted, he frowned and told me clearly that my friendship was not to be continued.

Around the same time, however, my mother's brother, who was stationed in Germany, came to visit us in the house on Donatusgasse. We were delighted to have my Uncle Bud, an Army Sergeant, in our home. Soon, though, Dad was questioned by his CO about "fraternizing with enlisted personnel." It didn't matter that said "enlisted personnel" was *his wife's brother.* Dad was pretty irritated about that but said nothing about it until years after he retired.

I was on a military shuttle bus that ran from the top of the hill to downtown Linz when two young soldiers attempted striking up a conversation. A few innocent questions, a mild flirtation, and then the bombshell—

"What's your dad's name?"

In that well-trained manner we Military Brats learn at an early age, I replied, "Captain R.M. Morris."

"Cheese it," one of the soldiers told the other, shaking his head ruefully. "Her dad's an officer."

Poor guys.

Poor me. They were cute.

An officer's kid could have been called a snob in the civilian world, but it was perfectly correct in the military environment to "stay with our own kind".

Languages:

Like many Brats, I learned "the local lingo" immediately upon arrival, even in the confines of the United States. If in Texas, I spoke with a drawl; in Kansas, I drew out my vowels in a nasal twang. When I transferred from Fort Hood TX to Fort Sill OK, my new friends teased me about my "Texas accent." I listened carefully and imitated their speech patterns. *Now that I'm a Texas resident, most people are surprised to hear my "non-Texas accent." Years of mimicry have led me to develop, in my later years, a homogenous speech pattern that is difficult for some to define.*

Of course, I chatted with the natives in their own languages. In Korea, a smattering of Korean phrases allowed me to communicate with the household help. In Austria, the language I spoke was a hodge-podge of Austro-German dialect with a bit of Hungarian/Romanian thrown in by the maid of the day. Textbook German was taught in school.

Years later, while on board a train from Germany to

Paris, I "conversed" in my limited German with a wonderful lady who knew no English. Using voluminous hand gestures, I told her that I had been a child of the US Military stationed in Austria after the War, and where I had lived. She told me the local military had knocked on their door one night and taken her father away, never to be seen again. We discussed religion and politics until we arrived at the Paris train station.

At least, I think we did....

Entertainment:

Besides reading, I enjoyed movies, which miraculously appeared on base wherever we were, including Korea. *Mother Wore Tights* enthralled me, while *Song of the South* had my little brother all wound up in the antics of Lumpjaw, the Bear. The theaters in Korea lacked a certain ambiance, of course—mostly they were little more than tents, with benches for seating. Once in a while, we attended a movie in downtown Seoul in a real movie theater but not often. We preferred the safety and familiarity of our compound.

"New" movies were warmly received as were records and books. Besides all that, we had our own Armed Forces Network radio programs. Even though the disc jockey played the very same records we already had, we listened anyway.I vividly remember a DJ in Korea named Chili Williams, whose lush voice no doubt caused homesick GI's a world of heartache. The Blue Danube Network in Austria, as far as I can remember, specialized in "re-up" commercials.

In Korea, we had an old, windup record player, and the

Red Cross provided records by the dozens, mostly songs made popular during World War II. I leaned heavily toward Glenn Miller and Harry James tunes, with some Crosby and Jimmy Dorsey thrown in: *Amapola, Green Eyes, Elmer's Tune, Tangerine, Sleepy Lagoon, Paper Doll, You'll Never Know, Besame Mucho* and *Swinging on a Star* (this tune played before the feature started at the El Paso movie theatre), to name just a few, playing them over and over.

In Linz, our facilities were more upscale. The Teen Club met a couple of nights a week for movies at The Gugelhof, a mansion formerly occupied by Nazi sympathizers.

One movie stands out vividly in my memory: *The Thing from Outer Space*—which pops up on television every now and then as one of the "classics." It certainly scared the dickens out of me, anyway, and each time I see it, I am reminded of the night when a group of us Military Brats missed the last bus and had to walk home.

Moving Itself:

Preparing to PCS came with startling regularity. Our longest stint was three years; many other tours were much shorter. We were allowed a certain weight for household goods, which meant some things had to be left behind. Many times, my mother sacrificed her own "favorite" items so that a bicycle or other item treasured by one of her kids could be loaded in our household goods.

Furniture rapidly became disposable. Mom managed to hang on to a few treasured items, but large pieces of furniture were either abandoned or given away before we departed.

As my mother and I stood on the deck of the *General Callan*, bound from Italy to the US, I watched in horror as a piano, being hauled up to the ship's deck, broke loose from its rigging and plunged into the bay.

"That's another reason not to own a piano." My mother, the minimalist, shurgged.

Preparing for Inspection, quarters were scrubbed, not just cleaned. We had put no holes in the regulation white walls, but handprints, any kind of soil, and imprints of scotch tape had to be covered. Cobwebs in window corners were erased and floors newly waxed. All in preparation for The Big Day when the movers came.

One widely circulated tale of movers/packers going beyond their usual duties is true. Numerous families, upon arriving at their new duty stations, unpacked their household goods, and found carefully wrapped ashtrays, complete with cigarette ashes.

Quarters:

We lived in quarters, not houses. In Korea, our address was HQ G27, in Camp Sobingo. Junction City, Kansas, was where we lived in a huge old house while Dad was stationed at Fort Riley. In Austria, we lived in three different areas: The first was "out of the American area" at #10 Donatusgasse; the second, in Bindermichel; and finally, Froschberg. For the most part, quarters were adequate and fairly comfortable. The apartment we were assigned in Bindermichel was probably the least favorite of all our quarters. Our apartment was a walk-up of three floors, and Mom was pregnant with my baby brother, Robert. I was in the 8th grade and *mortified* that *my mother* was *pregnant.*

Schools:

How many schools have I attended? Kindergarten in Lawton, OK; 1st grade in Fort Hancock, TX and Lawton, OK; 2nd grade at Lincoln Elementary; 3rd grade Whittier Elementary School, Lawton OK; remainder of 3rd and all of 4th grade, Seoul Dependents School, Seoul, Korea; 5th grade, Fort Riley KS (Junction City); 6th; 7th, & 8th grades, Linz Dependents School, Linz, Austria; 9th, Killeen High School, Killeen, TX (for all of about 2 weeks); transferred to Fort Hood High School; 10th, 11th, 12th grades, Lawton Sr. High, Lawton, OK. And two years of junior college at Cameron State College in Lawton OK.

Both my parents were avid readers, so I learned to read very early. I had also spent a lot of time with my grandparents and aunts and an uncle in West Texas, who, even though I was "the family baby" and my mother's Home Economics Project (she took me to school to show the class her latest sewing project—with me wearing it) never spoke "baby talk" to me.

I loved to read, and then I learned to write. Those

squiggle lines on the blackboard actually meant something—words. And thus, I was launched as a writer. English was my favorite subject with history a close second.

No matter where we were in the world, I knew one constant: school. Good, bad or indifferent as my father's assignments were, I always had school.

In the 4th grade, in Seoul, we studied Ancient History. I see even today my red textbook, chock full of exotic names: Mesopotamia, Tigris and Euphrates, Alexander the Great. When I read Alexander The Great cried because he had no more worlds to conquer, I was thoroughly entranced.

I carried books home every afternoon, did my homework sometimes by lantern-light, and wrote term papers. I got all A's. It was expected.

Teachers:

Mrs. Weed, and Mrs. Marcus, 4th grade in Seoul, Korea; Marjorie Otis, 6th grade, Linz; Sophie Schreiber, 7th & 8th grades; Frau Platzer, German teacher, Mrs. Betts, Home Economics, and Mr. Borne, who tried vainly to teach me math. Others too numerous to mention, their names lost in the shuttle from one school to another.

But I learned from them all.

Well, all except Mr. Borne.

Holidays:

Brats had lots of holidays, some of them unplanned, as our Russian neighbors rattled their sabers every so often. I relished the drama of racing from my schoolroom to board armed buses which whisked us back to our quarters every May Day. It never occurred to us to question why we even went to school on that date only to turn around and go back home.

Because we were military dependents, school was in session, and that was that.

I was in the 7th grade when I got the mumps during the Christmas holidays. Thoroughly miserable, I missed all the parties and casual get-togethers with my friends. Mother took this opportunity to force my kid brother Gary into my room hoping to expose him at an early age, but it didn't work. He has never had the mumps.

Our teachers took off on two-week trips to exotic places like Egypt and Morocco. That was one of the perks of being a teacher overseas, and most of them took full advantage of this time.

Travel by Ship:

One word: Seasick. Instantly. Every time. And for a long time.

We sailed from Fort Lawton, WA on the *USATGeneral Mayo* for Korea, returned on the *General Buckner* and returned from Austria via Italy on the *General Callan*.

Travel by Train:

Longest trip: From Oklahoma to Washington, where we boarded the ship to Korea.

Most hair-raising: In Europe: Encounters aboard the Orient Express, when Russian troops boarded and examined our papers with excruciating slowness.

Travel by Air:

Westover Field, Massachusetts, to Frankfurt, Germany, with stops in Newfoundland and the Azores. I got airsick.

Travel by Car:

I got carsick. During incessant days of fighting with my kid brother, we learned to watch for the Distant Early Warning System that Dad had had enough: The blood vessels on the back of Dad's neck stood out, and he was one nanosecond away from barking, "Do you want me to stop this car?"

Years later, as adults, my brothers and I were discussing "What would have happened if Dad *had* stopped the car?"

One brother said, "Well, ask him."

So I asked Dad, "What would you have done if you had actually had to stop the car?"

"I don't know," he shrugged.

"I never had to."

Dad preferred driving by night because it was cooler. This was before we had air-conditioned cars. We departed at 04:30, drove until it was time for breakfast (about 09:30) and then drove another couple of hundred miles before the afternoon heat assaulted us. On the rare occasions when no relatives were in the area, we began the search for a "clean" Tourist Court.

Dad checked out the rooms, and if he found anything he thought Mom wouldn't like (roaches, lumpy beds), we were out of there. Same with "greasy spoon" establishments for breakfasts and dinners. Food poisoning was a real concern after Gary and I ended up in a hospital in Wickenburg, Arizona, after eating eggs at a dubious-looking café somewhere along Route 66. This was one of the rare instances that prompted Dad to pause in his demonic driving. No matter how much my brother and I whined that we "gotta go," he stopped only to fill the car with gasoline. We learned to time our bladders to coincide with the fuel gauge. When it was nearly empty, we were on full.

All of our automobile travel was pre-interstate highway, much of it via the famous Route 66. Also, this era was pre-franchise eateries or motels. You took your chances each time you stopped as these were basically mom-and-pop operations, unregulated, and each one—well—unique. My mother's radar was pretty good at spotting those places where she would allow us to eat or sleep. But at certain points, we were caught with no choice but to stay in "a fleabag" or eat at a "greasy spoon." Whenever Mom entered a dubious-looking establishment, her lips became tighter. I soon began to think of this look as "The Garrett Grimace;" like my Grandpa Garrett, thin lipped already, showed his displeasure by drawing his lips together so they almost disappeared. So it was with my mother. This was *her DEW line.*

When we traversed the American Southwest Desert, Dad hung a burlap water bag on the front of the car; explaining that this cooled the radiator. I wasn't interested in the technical aspects, but just appreciated the fact that it provided the best-tasting, coolest water I ever drank.

As we were traversing the Great American Southwest Desert during one of Dad's many PCSs, I realized we were pretty close to The Grand Canyon, and one of my heart's desires was to spit in the Grand Canyon. I don't know where or how I got that idea, but it burned in my gut, so much so, that I dared to ask Dad if we could go see The Grand Canyon.

"That's one hundred miles out of the way," he snorted.

I screwed up my face and whined again. After a few minutes of this, Mom's countenance gradually changed into The Garrett Grimace, before she finally snapped, "Oh, for heavens sakes! Let Marilyn spit in the Grand Canyon."

And so, at dawn, with the magnificent sunrise casting shadows on the deep gorge, Dad pulled our trusty vehicle to a lookout point, I got out, walked to the edge and spat.

"Okay, let's go." Dad said. "We're way behind schedule."

Gary and I sat in the back seat, sometimes ensconced on the "bed" that we built up with suitcases and blankets, making a level surface for sleeping. But since my assigned task was to keep Mom awake so she could keep Dad awake, I couldn't sleep. *To this day, I cannot sleep in a car.*

I sat as close to the front of the car as I could so I could talk to my parents and hear the radio over the wind whistling through the open windows. This meant that my feet were constantly propped on the "hump" (the transmission) where they roasted. *Today if my feet are hot, I am miserable and cannot sleep.*

A word about motion sickness, something I have recently discovered. I believe that much of the motion sickness I suffered was caused, in part, by fear. I had merely to look at a ship bobbing innocently in the harbor, and smell the brackish water mixed with oil and various flotsam and jetsam, and my queasy stomach heaved. The prospect of boarding an airplane or anticipating a long car trip sent my innards churning.

Probably, I was fearful of what I might find on the other end of the trip. I have since been aboard small vessels without getting seasick—if the seas are calm. Very calm. Although I still don't like to fly, I have found that sitting in a window seat helps my equilibrium, and I try to schedule my flight during daylight hours. Of course, all bets are off if there's any kind of turbulence, at all.

And if I'm going someplace in a car, I prefer to drive, or at least sit in the front seat. My brothers torment me mercilessly when we go see our mother: "Sis always has to sit in the front seat." So one of my long-legged, 6'2" brothers has to sit doubled up in the back seat. Sorry, guys.

Staying at relatives' homes along the way from one post to another:

"Relatives" could mean anyone from a one of my mother's sisters to a very distant cousin from my grandfather's first marriage. It didn't matter. We were made welcome and provided clean, comfortable accommodations from coast to coast.

The Issue of Drinking:

My dad drank. My mom drank. All their friends drank at parties, at the Officers' Club, and at home. In Austria, we had parties on the lawn where beer kegs were drained with astonishing swiftness. In Korea, personnel were issued a certain amount of liquor: so many bottles of whiskey, so many of vodka, vermouth, etc. If Scotch was your weakness, you could always trade with some buddy who preferred Jack Daniels.

One of my memories of Korea was waking one morning after my parents had hosted a party and finding two or three "Officers and Gentlemen" passed out on the couch, the overstuffed chair, and even on the cold hardwood floor. Three-year-old Gary cruised the scene, picking up half-empty beer bottles and draining the last few swallows. If he ever had a hangover the next day, I didn't know about it. And he doesn't drink today—he's a Mormon.

Drinking was not only accepted, it was almost encouraged as part of the camaraderie, upheld by the military's long tradition. Their wives were not discouraged either. Their husbands off on maneuvers, their children in school and after school being looked after by houseboys/house girls/maids or other household staff, some women sought refuge from their boredom in playing bridge at the Officers' Club or their quarters and more than a few wives succumbed to alcoholism.

I can still see my mother playing bridge with one immaculately groomed hand while her other held a glass of beer or another alcoholic drink. She painted her long fingernails and dressed up to go either to the Club or to some other woman's house. When she wasn't involved in bridge, she read or listened to music.

She was also a pretty good artist, at least where drawing paper dolls was concerned. She drew a shapely woman in a bathing suit, which I cut out, and then, she drew various dresses for her, complete with tabs to press on the paper doll.

I have always been grateful that my mother hadn't spent her time drinking like many of the women in the compound, and that she had a great inner strength to draw upon while living such a tedious life in such a far-away place.

Brats as being "loners":

I've been categorized by some as "a loner"—a phrase I've bristled at. I enjoy the company of good friends, coworkers, others. I also enjoy my own company, and at times, I am perfectly content to stay by myself all day, reading or, more importantly, writing. This ease of being alone, but not lonely, sprang from—what else—my childhood.

I spent a great deal of time alone, particularly in Korea, where I was confined to the compound with few other children my age around to play with. Of course, we gathered for softball games, played on our quarter's bare yard, and our school provided essential social contact, but much of the time, I was alone. Rather than feeling sorry for myself on frigid winter nights, or torrid summer days, I read or was read to or wrote stories or drew. At one point, I took an old wooden crate and turned it into a dollhouse complete with a pipe-cleaner picket fence and pocket mirror swimming pool. Curtains were courtesy of the Sears, Roebuck catalogue, and the furniture was made of shaped cardboard.

Being alone so much as a child strengthened me for my later adulthood when my first husband was away on business all week, and when another husband was away drinking all night, and finally, when I disentangled myself to live as a single woman, at last relishing the freedom and its accompanying solitude. After a busy week at work, I crave a long weekend spent in near-solitude.

Alone, yes. Lonely, never.

My History
as a Brat

My father called us "gypsies":

From 1938, when I entered the world in my maternal grandfather's house, until 1958, when our family stood on the cold, windy Polo Field at Fort Sill, Oklahoma, watching Dad's retirement ceremony with a strange mixture of pride and wrenching sadness, we traversed the globe. From Fort DA Russell, Texas, to Fort Bragg, North Carolina, we criss-crossed the map of the United States, weary, apprehensive, and always, always, in Dad's latest automobile, more than likely a Ford. At other times, we were subjected to transport via ship, train and plane, to far-flung exotic lands—Korea (or Chosen as it was listed on our travel vouchers) and Europe—and not-so-exotic lands, such as Fort Riley, Kansas, and Fort Hood, Texas.

My father was an Officer in the US Army. In the parlance of the US Army, my mother, my kid brother Gary Wayne and later, my brother Robert Lynn, born in Austria, and I, were labeled "Dependents."

THE AUTHOR WITH HER FATHER AND BROTHER
CIRICA 1944

Dependents we were.

We depended on Dad's orders, which arrived exactly as I was finally adjusting to yet another school in yet another country/state/city. We depended on the US Army to arrange our travel, to provide us with food, clothing, shelter and other necessities of life. We lived in primitive conditions and in luxurious surroundings. We toured castles, explored Hitler's hide-aways and foraged in attics haunted by the ghosts of Nazis past.

The constant travel both thrilled me and made me ill. I got carsick, seasick, airsick, and if ordered to travel by ox-cart, I would no doubt have become cart-sick.

I saw men urinating in the streets of Seoul, Korea. As our train slowed to a crawl in rubble-strewn Frankfurt in 1949, I watched refugees forage in trash barrels. And, at the end of the Korean War, my father sent pictures of our former quarters in Seoul, which had been pockmarked and strafed; the windows boarded.

I loved it, and I hated it.

I adjusted, and I didn't adjust.

Before I entered another new school in another new country, or in another new town, I stood in front of the bathroom mirror, practicing my smiles. Should I smile my "Girl Scout" smile? Should I not smile? Should I look mysterious? What to wear? Do girls in this school wear Peter Pan collars?

I wonder if they're studying fractions or decimals. Despite my Military Dependents School education, I was sadly lacking in math skills. Somewhere between Korea and Junction City, Kansas, decimals must have fallen into the Pacific. I could identify countries on the globe; I could read at an adult level from the third grade on; I was a champion speller and a dedicated Ancient History buff, but I couldn't figure percentages.

I spoke a smattering of Austro-German mixed with refugees' Rumanian and Czech, and when these phrases slipped naturally out of my mouth in Killeen High School, Texas, I was laughed at. I crawled out of one class, totally humiliated. (Never mind that these were kids who confused

Austria with *Australia.*) About the third or fourth week of constantly being ridiculed, when I trudged home in tears, again, Mom and Dad threw up their hands in defeat, and we moved—to another area of Killeen where I was eligible to attend Fort Hood Dependents School -- I was back "with my own kind."

It wasn't until I was grown and with children of my own that I came to realize that my childhood had not been what I thought it had been. That is, I had been indoctrinated by my parents–albeit innocently—to believe that I loved the advantages this nomadic life afforded me: the world travel, the immersion in Eastern cultures one year, the next two, I was learning the ways of the Europeans. In one of those fleeting "deja-vu" experiences as I was telling an acquaintance about my Military Brat background, my mind flashed back to the following scene: My mother and I are chatting with one of her friends, no doubt a bridge-playing partner, when the woman turns to me and says brightly, "Well, Marilyn, I suppose all the travel and changing schools must have had an impact on you. Did you enjoy it?" I opened my mouth to speak, when I felt my mother's hand on my arm, exerting a firm, warning pressure, as she spoke for me.

"Oh, she loved it!"

I thought in astonishment, "I did?"

Emotions flooded over me. Resentment, anger, a keen sense of loss over things I had never experienced—Never living in one house, going to one grade school, then one junior high school, with the same kids I went to first grade with, watching my friends grow up, begin dating, saying hello to my teachers in the supermarket when I was grown, with my own children ready to be taught by these same teachers....

Grief flooded over me, not for the childhood I had, but for the childhood I never had.

I entered therapy about that time. My second marriage was ending, and this seemed to be yet another reason for getting help. My emotions were riding a roller coaster, anyway, and every arrow through my heart hit a bulls-eye on an old wound from my Military Brat days.

Was it all bad? No, of course not. Neither was it the Fairy Tale I had been led to believe—and, in all fairness— I had manufactured my own Fairy Tales, so I could deny the reality of my world, and in my fantasies, I was a Princess and lived in a castle.

As early as three years of age, I had endowed my parents with royalty—when my father dressed for a formal evening affair, he looked every bit the part of a Prince of some exotic land, complete with ribbons on his chest, Sam Browne belt glistening in the lamplight, and those regulation jodhpurs and high leather boots.

My mother, when she appeared, was certainly Cinderella on her way to the ball, if not Sleeping Beauty and Rapunzel wrapped in one. Tall and willowy with long black hair cascading down her back, she had chosen her gown carefully to complement her dark beauty: an off the shoulder yellow chiffon, scoop neck to reveal her regal neck, fluffy cap sleeves, a nipped-in waist, and—the pièce de résistance: large black lace butterflies appliquéd around the full hem.

Never mind that we lived in Lawton, Oklahoma, in a small rented house with linoleum floors; at that instant, my parents were King and Queen making me at least a Princess in my own kingdom.

As I lay seasick on my bunk in the middle of the Pacific Ocean, on my way to God knows where, I dreamed of a perfect house, warm and cheerful; what we were presented with was a perfectly vanilla military quarters with no running water.

After landing in Frankfurt in 1949 and taking the Orient Express into Austria, my fantasy was that our butler would meet my family and me at the train and would whisk us away to a smaller version of a castle, but a castle nonetheless. But when we arrived, we were herded onto a creaky old jeep and dumped at an ancient, drafty hotel where we promptly contracted diarrhea, and the bathroom was yards away down the hall.

My whole life had been like that, I mused in therapy. I grew to understand that it wasn't the unusual circumstances of my life, but it was my perception—my expectations—that caused the pain.

I blocked it out by reading, listening to old records, and denying what was actually taking place. The little Princess in me had felt betrayed somehow, if not by her father (the King) and mother (the Queen) then by The Army—Her God.

This God was a vengeful, punishing God, who would take her father away from her if she didn't behave . . . only nobody was telling the Princess the rules—what does "behave" mean, anyway? I knew in my bones that I had to obey. If the Daily Bulletin had said that I had to wear purple socks on Tuesdays, I would have worn purple socks on Tuesdays . . . no questions asked. I just followed orders like my father followed orders.

The Big Bad God did take the King away. The Army snatched him away one day when I was in the third grade at Whittier Elementary School in Lawton, Oklahoma.

My daddy hadn't had to go off to the War. When the war ended, Dad was in flight training at Shepard AFB in Texas. Mom, Gary, and I were in Alpine that summer when we heard the fire station's siren going off, then, church bells. Running outside, we saw a little Hispanic boy, barefoot on the hot asphalt, racing across the railroad tracks toward the middle of town. "What is it? What's happening?" we asked.

"The war is over!" he panted, never breaking his stride. "The war is over!"

"Thank God," we breathed as one.

Now Daddy won't have to go away, I thought.

But the Army had other plans. He was ordered to the Far East, where we would join him later.

I came home from school one day, and he was gone.

I went to my parent's bedroom—my mother's bedroom, now—and sought out the portrait of my father in uniform. His handsome face gazed out at me.

"Oh, Daddy!" Huge tears ran down my face and much to my horror, onto my father's picture. Panicked, I traced the tears down his face with my fingers, which only led to streaks, which are still visible today.

Oh, well, the harm was done, I thought, and I continued to weep and shed more tears onto the portrait.

I didn't know it at the time, but I felt abandoned, betrayed, and angry. Angry that my father had gone—again. It was to be a pattern repeated for many years until my father's death. I thought, somehow, I could have prevented his leaving. I had been a "bad" girl. If only I had been better, brighter, prettier, etc., etc., the King would not have left me.

And I was left in the care of the Queen, who might abandon me, too. So I toed the line, behaved myself, all the while wishing to rebel against my restrictions, but not being quite brave enough. All I could manage in the way of rebellion was to be a bit "sassy" to my mother.

And that didn't work too well, either.

My friend down the street talked back to her mother, stamping her foot, and saying "No!" Her mother backed down. Wow, I thought. I think I'll try that.

The next time Mother told me to do something, I stamped my foot and said, "No!"

The Queen's green eyes flashed and she pointed her long, painted fingernail at me: "Go to your room!"

Well, that didn't work, I pouted.

While waiting for our orders, I went to school, Gary was busy being a three year-old, and Mom coped—playing bridge with neighbors and writing long letters to her mother in West Texas, who begged us to come home for a while before we left for the Orient.

But Mother was reluctant to take us there during the school year, and besides, I had the Lead in the School Play: *Marjorie's Christmas Dinner*.

As Marjorie, I was supposed to have fallen asleep and dreamed about the Christmas dinner dancing around—salt and pepper shakers danced and sang while I, regally clad in new pajamas, slippers, and bathrobe, observed. The day before my performance, my teacher sent me home, telling my mother in a stage whisper that she thought I might be experiencing a bit of stage fright.

What nobody knew at that time, and I didn't connect the two events until years later, was that some kid had sneered that my father wouldn't be there to see me in my performance. Nor would he be there for many other performances in many years to come, I might add. That was just the way it was.

While waiting for our port call, Mom, Gary and I made regular trips to Fort Sill for our inoculations. A regular laundry list of exotic diseases called for excruciatingly painful shots. Japanese B Encephalitis was one that made grown men tremble and faint. My arm stung like a bee, but that was preferable over the typhoid shots, which made my arm feel like lead, hot and feverish, for days. The tetanus shot was my next least favorite series of inoculations; mercifully, I have blotted out memories of many others such as cholera and plague.

Finally, our passport picture was made. We look like refugees: a mother with two children, a three-year old boy in her lap. She is gazing at the camera as if to say, "I am a woman alone who is preparing to go to the ends of the earth to join my husband." The little boy is wide-eyed, a puzzled frown on his brow; and me, the eight-year old? My eyes are dull and vacant communicating what I must have been feeling: *I have been abandoned by my father and I want to cry but I can't.*

At last, a letter from my father arrived.

As Mother opened the envelope, a small map fell out; she picked it up absently and began reading the letter aloud: "I am in Chosen, or Korea, as it is called now."

"Korea?" Mother wailed. "Where is that?"

I pointed to the map as Mother continued to read, her voice shaking with fear: "Korea is a peninsula off the coast of China, across the sea from Japan."

And there it was, dangling like a forgotten apostrophe, off the coast of Manchuria. *Manchuria,* for God's sake!

"*Korea.*"

I joined her in wailing, loud and long.

Around this time, I learned of a neighboring woman who was also anticipating her port call. Only this woman did not want to go. So she chose the only way out that she could think of.

On Halloween, neighbors out supervising their trick-or-treaters found her two young children outside, coatless and crying in the cold night. The doors to her house were locked, and after unsuccessfully trying to contact the mother, they called the police. She was found dead on the kitchen floor, a gunshot wound to her head.

I listened to the rumors and whispers and deduced that if you can't cope, you die. When I got a divocre (I was "abadoned"), I thought I couldn't cope, and the thought of that woman choosing death over change haunted me.

My mother's option was to cope. She had coped all her life. So why couldn't I?

So I chose to cope, and the specter of the fallen woman vanished.

In the first part of a new year, 1947, our travel orders arrived. Very official, very Army, and very misspelled, at least where my mother's name was concerned: "Franc*is*" Garrett Morris, Marilyn Celeste Morris, and Gary Wayne Morris, Dependents. But my mother Franc*es* was just grateful to get the orders, misspelled name or not.

But that summer Mother decided to join her two married sisters in Fort Hancock, Texas, where my grandparents lived at that time. I became accustomed to the arrivals and departures of the Southern Pacific trains; the house in Marfa sat so close to the tracks that the house vibrated when the engines roared by. I learned to sleep soundly through the noise.

Trains were part of my mother's life and to a lesser degree, mine. Mom's father, Felix Garrett, had two former occupations before he signed up with the Southern Pacific Railroad: He had been a cowboy and was an Indian Agent in Ajo, Arizona, where he met and married my grandmother, Emily Richardson. Emily, half Papago Indian, stood almost eye-to-eye with my six-foot tall grandfather. They produced one child, my mother, Martha Frances, before Emily's tragic death from a ruptured appendix.

My grandfather had few options for taking care of a three-year old girl, so he departed for Denver on business, leaving Frances in the care of the Richardsons.

He returned with a new wife, Fern Herrmann, and began his career with the Southern Pacific Railroad. His assignments as a Section Foreman took him to Toronto, Texas, six miles from Alpine, Texas, and that is where I was born in my grandfather's house, April 21, 1938.

Frances Garrett had met a handsome young soldier from nearby Fort DA Russell, who courted her—and her family—by jumping onto the train (free, of course—as any young man in uniform attained such privileges)—riding to a point where the train slowed for a long, curved section of track, and jumped off, walking the rest of the way to my grandfather's section house.

My grandparents were against one of their daughters dating a soldier, especially when war loomed, but when they saw the couple was determined to get married, with or without their permission, they relented.

Frances Garrett, age 17, and Rawlins Marion "Wayne" Morris, age 18, were married in the Parsonage of the First Methodist Church in Alpine, Texas on Wednesday, June 30, 1937.

It was payday, of course.

My Aunt Olivia, Mother's younger sister, and her young son, Jimmy, were already in Fort Hancock when we arrived. My Aunt Joyce was in San Angelo, in nursing school and my Aunt Mary (three years my senior) and Uncle Bud (at that time in high school) still living at home, completed the crowd. Yet we managed. Bud, Mary and I slept in the attic room; Mother, Olivia, and their sons occupied a downstairs bedroom while Grandma and Grandpa slept outside on the large, screened sleeping porch.

Meals were a treat, turned out on Grandma's venerable wood-burning stove. At the large table, in the mornings, we could choose from a bounty of oatmeal, bacon, eggs, or pancakes. Lunch was on our own; often, we would have left-overs from breakfast, such as a rolled up pancake, slathered with fresh butter and sugar and more bacon. Dinner consisted of some kind of meat dish or beans with fresh vegetables and cornbread. Grandpa insisted we taste everything, or he would set his thin lips in a straight line, a signal that we grandchildren had pushed him too far. My mother would inherit this "Garrett Grimace;" I'm certain I have also adopted this practice.

All of these meals were accompanied by fresh milk— straight from the cow herself—which I hated to look at first thing in the morning, with steam rising in the cold air.

During the day, a large part of my chores consisted of churning butter; I thought my arm would fall off before the butter set. Our eggs were fresh, too. My grandparents maintained a small brood of chickens in a well-built chicken house. Another of my jobs was to gather the eggs from under the setting hens. I hated that chore, too because the old hens pecked my hand as it attempted to rob the hen of her precious egg.

Washday was Monday, and I dreaded it.

First, the black kettle full of water was set over a fire in the side yard while one of the girls shaved a cake of lye soap into the water. Clothes were added gradually, stirred with a broomstick, then plucked out of the boiling water and dumped in a galvanized tub of rinse water. We had to wring the items by hand, then put them in a basket for hanging on the line.

Part of my job was to hang the clothes on the clothesline, which stretched from the side of the house across the vast side yard into infinity. The clothesline was propped up in the middle with a large stick set into the hard West Texas ground.

The wind was usually blowing, and when I came to hanging Grandpa's work clothes on the line, I prayed the wind would stop, just for a little while. But it usually didn't, so I stuck the denim overalls onto the line, secured them with clothespins, and *ducked.*

Grandpa's overalls had huge brass buckles that *hurt* when slapped across my tender face. I hurried as fast as I could with my portion of the laundry-hanging, looking for the tell-tale signs of the end of wash day when I saw Grandma pouring the rinse water on the spindly flowers; the wash pot water would be used later, when it cooled, to scrub the front porch.

That is, washday would be over *if* one of the boys, racing through the yard, didn't kick out the stick supporting the clothesline. If they did, the clothes would tumble to the dirt, and washday would start all over again.

It wasn't all work at my grandparents' house. I watched trains rumble past and blimps glide silently overhead. The rest of my days were spent in a tree house or giving a tarantula a Christian burial (after first killing him with mercy, of course.)

Since it was post-war time, and nylon stockings were scarce, my mother and her sisters spent many hours outside, in their shorts, "painting" nylon stockings on each other, complete with straight "seam" down the back.

We didn't know it at the time, of course, but all the "hardships" of cooking on a wood-burning stove, storing food in an ice box and sometimes pumping water, even the fashion substitutes would serve us well when we arrived in Korea.

My grandmother often took the grandchildren to El Paso on daylong trips, which were magical in my eyes. Packing a huge lunch basket, we boarded the train early in the morning, arrived in El Paso in time to do a little shopping, and perhaps take in a movie before the long ride back. The gentle swaying of the cars and the clickety clack of wheels on the rails that I knew my grandpa had worked on lulled me to sleep long before we reached home.

We packed and boarded a train in Lawton, Oklahoma, bound for Bremerton, Washington, and the ship that would take us across the vast Pacific to the exotic Far East.

This train trip was seemingly unending. From Lawton, Oklahoma, we traversed ever northwestward switching trains at least twice, fearing our luggage would not be forwarded to the appropriately bound train, and Mother wrestling with the decision of how much to tip the Red Caps who cheerfully hauled our bags off and on.

Overnights, once a novelty, soon became customary in this journey. Mom and Gary slept on the bottom berth and I took the top. Once I drew the curtain closed, it became my very own sanctuary. My belongings placed in the little hammock-like nets, I daydreamed of our destination.

What would it be like? Would I make new friends there? Daddy had told me there would be a school, so I imagined there would be somebody my age, at least.

After the novelty of venturing time after time up to the front of the car and holding a "pointy" paper cup under the cold water cooler and drinking it down immediately because the pointy end wouldn't allow you to set it down, wore off, daytime on the train soon became wearying. My three-year-old brother Gary and I competed with each other to see who could drink the most in the least amount of time. Close by the water coolers were the bathrooms or the "ladies' lounge" or "men's room" where everyone washed up and changed into nightwear.

We encountered our fellow passengers strolling down the aisle in bathrobes and slippers, and the parade continued in the morning as everyone got dressed for the day. One night, I attempted to undress in the top berth; by the time I finished thrashing around, hitting my elbows on all three sides of the compartment, I gave that up and returned to dressing and undressing in the "ladies' lounge."

At each stop along the way, we had an opportunity to alight from the train even if only for a few moments to buy a newspaper or a sandwich from one of the "butchers" who hawked his wares along the station's tracks.

Mother decreed that we would not purchase from these vendors, since they might not be too clean, and then, we would all get sick. (This was even *before* the "food poisoning from eating at a greasy spoon" incident.)

She preferred that we eat our meals in the dining car. There was nothing particularly memorable in the dining car's menu from my kid's perspective, but Mother seemed to find it very good. The white tablecloths, uniformed waiters, good china, silver and glassware seemed to soothe the adults' psyches while it only hampered the children's enjoyment. This was just another dinner table where we had to mind our manners.

At last, we reached Fort Lewis, Washington. Wearily, we filed into a hotel for the night and fell into beds that didn't move. After a hasty breakfast, our fellow passengers gathered to hear their instructions for travel on board the *USAT General Mayo*. As I climbed the gangway, my stomach churned. We were assigned a cabin on "D" Deck, way down below, which was dark, dank and dreary, and had no portholes. It was below the waterline.

As the *Mayo* pulled away from Fort Lewis, Mom, Gary and I promptly became seasick. Terribly, horribly, continually seasick. I smelled cabbage boiling in the galley, and to this day, I feel nauseated whenever I encounter that particular odor. Sympathetic crewmen ventured into our odiferous cabin and placed large trashcans beside our bunks. Dispelling the notion that seasickness is all in the head, Gary threw up even in his sleep.

I tried not to move, yet every time the ship tossed, I heaved.

Mother alternately moaned and vomited.

After what seemed like weeks, Mom rallied and ordered us onto the deck where we breathed deeply of the crisp, salty air.

For the first time since we left port, we ate dinner, and managed to keep everything down. My mother found three other bridge players, and they would begin meeting daily in the Lounge. Gary played with other three-year olds, and I found a girl about my age to talk to. Maybe we would survive this voyage after all.

A Boat Drill was scheduled the next day

As bells clanged, we put on our life vests and rushed to our assigned stations. The boys found these "Mae Wests" just dandy to butt against one another, and proceeded to crash about the bulkheads, while the girls mulled over the possibilities of someday having chests of that massive size.

Fortunately, our mothers paid attention to the life boat instructions.

Soon our ship was passing the Aleutian Islands, and despite it being February in the North Pacific, everyone gathered on deck to gaze wistfully at these pieces of land almost hidden by the choppy waters.

We crossed the International Date Line, where we experienced the loss of one complete day—we went from Sunday to Tuesday, by-passing Monday altogether. On our return trip, we would be fortunate enough to celebrate not one, but two, July 4ths. We were given impressive-looking certificates with King Neptune as the central figure, but fortunately, we would not perform the age-old ritual of being "dunked" in the ocean. I suspect that my father and other soldiers, crossing the Pacific earlier on the Gallant, probably participated in that, and other rituals.

The ship's crew did their best to keep us informed and entertained on this long, tedious voyage. They issued a Daily Bulletin listing not only what movie was scheduled each evening, but also provided a concise report of what was happening in "the real world."

One night, a talent show was on tap and everyone was urged to participate. A couple of women sang; someone played the piano, and another girl and I concocted a silly routine. The premise was that our slacks pockets were so full of junk that when someone asked us for a piece of gum, we pulled out yards and yards of material only to discover we had no gum. I'm sure we eight-year-old girls thought we were the epitome of humor.

I'm equally sure the applause that followed was prompted only by relief that our act was over.

The closer we came to Japan, the more we encountered floating mines, which looked to me as if they were awfully close to our ship. I stood on deck watching them glide safely by—but there was always another one, it seemed. After some ten or twelve days, we assumed the majority of passengers would disembark at Japan. Envy flooded over me that they would be getting off this ship, no more seasickness, no more cold, biting sea wind, and they would feel firm ground under their feet once more.

But we were wrong.

Those bound for *Korea* would be the first to disembark.

Maps were magically produced, and we traced the route: Around the islands into the Sea of Japan, and our destination was oh, so close.

Pusan, on the southern end of the Korean peninsula would have been the logical port.

Not noted for its logic, however, the military plan was to sail up the coastline to Inchon, on the northwest coast.

The ship seemed to stand still on this final leg of our voyage. Reaching her goal at last, the *USAT General Mayo* sighed and dropped anchor.

As we assembled on deck, we were told Inchon Harbor was not deep enough to accommodate a ship this size; therefore, we would be transported to the dock via LCTs (Landing Craft Tanks). *Just like we had seen in newsreels, where soldiers clambered down rope ladders into smaller craft that took them to shore, and then the big doors would open and armed troops ran onto shore.*

Our faces must have shown consternation, anxiety, and fear. The captain assured us we would not use ropes over the side but ladders. Young crewmen assisted every frightened woman and child down the ladders, and two or three small babies were gently handed down to the crewmen waiting below.

Soon, we were all standing in the smaller craft.

I looked up at the brilliant blue sky. A warming sun partially eliminated the bitter cold as we slowly motored toward shore.

I jumped as something thumped against the hull.

"Ice floes," a crewman said with a reassuring smile. "We'll hit more of 'em before we get to the dock."

Although the sides of this new craft were too high for even the tallest person among us to see over them, all faces were turned expectantly toward land.

Except for the ship's engine and the occasional "thump" and "whack" of ice floes scraping the hull, the only sound was a child's whimper, then a yell of protest as I wiped Gary's nose for the hundredth time.

"Be quiet," I said irritably, and pinched his nose for good measure.

Daddy might not recognize us, I thought. *He's been gone for almost a year, and I'm bigger. Gary's grown, too. Mother's lost so much weight she's skin and bones.*

And I, putting on a brave face, must have appeared old beyond my years.

I felt the craft bump something else.

It must be the dock. The engines stopped.

A hush fell.

Then we heard a military band begin playing, *"Kiss Me Once and Kiss Me Twice, and Kiss Me Once Again, It's Been a Long, Long Time."*

A cheer went up, both onshore and inside the craft, as the huge gates creaked open.

Like Jonah's whale, women and children spewed forth onto dry land..

Pushed along by the crowd, Mom, Gary and I passed dozens of families embracing and crying with joy under a huge sign that read: *"Welcome to Inchon. Best Damn Port in the Pacific."*

Women's shrill cries and men's hearty laughter filled my ears. I smelled the familiar odors of damp wool uniforms, Brasso, shaving lotion and cigarette smoke.

I watched as reunited families, mothers and fathers, their children between them, drifted away.

Where is Daddy?

We were standing alone on the dock. Turning to my mother, I saw her face echoing my unspoken fear: *He's*

not here. We came all this way, and he's not here. Something's happened to him.

Then, I saw her break into a smile of recognition and relief as a uniformed figure sprinted toward us. We were immediately enveloped in a bear hug with me squeezed between my parents and my little brother squirming alongside.

Daddy's here.

Everything will be all right, now.

After a moment, when we had finished laughing and crying at the same time, we recovered our breath.

I wiped Gary's nose again. This time, he didn't yell.

"You've grown," Dad said to both Gary and me.

I nodded.

Scooping Gary up in his arms, Dad gestured, "We go this way. We're going into Seoul on a train."

I looked at several passenger cars pulled by a very old steam engine as we hurried toward them.

Settling into the few vacant seats, our fellow passengers already seated, the train lurched into a faint pull, then gained momentum.

A few short moments later, however, the train screeched and bumped to a halt.

"They're working on the tracks," someone explained.

"Just like Grandpa's work," I said to Gary as we stood at the windows.

One of the workers turned toward the train, grinned and casually urinated on the tracks.

I'm sure my jaw dropped.

"Mom!" I hissed.

My brother harrumphed as only an outraged three-year-old can:

"Ummmm! Mama, you told me never to do that outside!"

The other passengers laughed, and Gary looked puzzled.

"This is common, ordinary, and accepted," Dad said.

Thus began our orientation into the ways of other people in a foreign country.

Dad continued telling us some of the other local customs.

"People here do things we don't. Like what you just saw. For instance, if they enjoy a meal, it's considered a compliment if you belch."

Gary grinned and burped loudly.

"Not now, son.

"And you might hear some of the GIs calling the Koreans '*Gooks*.' That's not allowed. You're never to say it, understand?"

We nodded our heads.

"When we first came to this country, the Koreans kept saying, '*Migook, Migook*'—that means us . . . Americans. But some of the soldiers thought that was funny; like the Koreans were saying, '*Me, a Gook.*' So the GIs started calling them '*Gooks.*'

"Which isn't right. Okay? The people here may not have things we have back in the States, but that doesn't make them stupid. They're just different, and different doesn't mean stupid. So don't ever treat them that way."

Gary and I nodded again.

"Yes, Sir," I added almost forgetting and prompted Gary with a tap; we certainly had not said "Yes, *Ma'am*" to our poor mother in Dad's absence.

Wrapped in the warmth of the passenger car, combined with the rocking of the train, Gary was soon lulled to sleep.

Although I fought valiantly, I fell asleep, too.

"Marilyn, wake up. We're here," I heard my mother saying.

I was not a "leap from my cot" type of person, and waking me from a nap generally resulted in others wishing I were still asleep; I was so irritable. This time was no exception.

I must have said something really "sassy" as my father's swift hand sent me sprawling across the seat in the opposite aisle.

I had been a holy terror to my mother while my father was gone. Perhaps I was angry with her for my father having gone away, but more likely, I was just a typical

75

eight-year old girl who took advantage of her father's absence to inflict as much irritation on her mother as possible.

Now, Dad had smacked me, the first and only time I remember his raising a hand to me.

"You will not sass your mother."

"Yes, Sir," I mumbled, my hand feeling my cheek.

And I didn't sass my mother—anymore—especially when my dad was around.

Properly subdued, I followed Dad to a waiting jeep; its canvas sides zipped up against the freezing temperature. We four clambered in and set out through the narrow streets of the capital city.

Ox carts, bicycles, pedicabs, trolley cars, stray animals and unconcerned pedestrians clogged the streets. The odor of animal and human excrement, urine, smoke from open-air vendors' hibachis, decaying fish and fermented cabbage combined in one nauseating stench.

"You'll get used to all this," Dad said.

Mother, however, dug into her purse for her perfumed handkerchief and held it over her nose.

I had used my handkerchief on my brother, and I was loath to even bring it out of my pocket, so I held my breath as long as I could. That didn't work too well, so I just pinched my nose and breathed through my mouth.

We were soon on an open stretch of road that led us into a military compound.

The guard at the entry gate saluted as we passed.

"This is Camp Sobingo," Dad said.

"The Commissary is over there," Dad gestured. "Sis, your school is that big building down that way."

I looked at the huge domed building and gulped. Gee, it was the biggest school I'd ever seen.

Fear assaulted me again.

"The Dispensary is over there.

"And this is the housing area," he said as he made a sweeping turn.

Befitting a military compound, all the quarters looked alike: small, square houses of stucco, a stoop in front, a yard now covered with deep snow, and a few spindly, bare trees.

Dad pulled the jeep into a gravel driveway beside one of the structures.

"This is ours."

And the requisite sign in the front of the yard confirmed it: HQ G27, RM Morris, Capt.

The front door opened, and a young Korean man bounded outside, grinning and nodding.

"Sah, Captain, Sah."

"This is our houseboy, Kim. He speaks a little English."

Kim began grabbing our luggage, bowing and grinning, his eyes lighting up at the sight of Gary.

"Ah, ichi bon, Sah. Numbah One Son."

Another foreign custom.

"Only Gary matters," I muttered under my breath, "because he's a boy."

I bristled as we followed Dad into the house.

We entered directly into the living/dining area, which contained a small amount of non-descript furniture: A couch, a couple of overstuffed chairs, two end tables and lamps.

The dining area was furnished with a large mahogany table and six chairs; a huge matching china cabinet held an exquisite service for twelve, courtesy of the Japanese government as part of reparations. That would be the only spot of beauty in the place until we received our household goods.

From the living room, a door led into a hallway. A linen closet and houseboy's room were almost immediately in front of us; the master bedroom was on the left. My room was at the end of the hall.

It had two windows—one on the north and one on the west.

I was happy.

Along this central corridor was what would be Gary's room and the bathroom.

Oh, oh, I thought as I peered inside the bathroom.

I glanced at my mother waiting for her reaction.

The bathroom contained a lidless toilet equipped with a water tank near the ceiling and a pull-chain. Next to the toilet was a brown-stained sink. Opposite, an open tiled area with a tank at the top pretended to be a shower stall.

Mother, to her credit, did not faint. Or cry.

Not just yet.

At the other end of the hallway was a door to the kitchen.

An image of my mother's facial expression is burned in my memory as she surveyed the kitchen.

Frances Garrett Morris had married and escaped a harsh West Texas environment, in her parents' house with "four rooms and a path." It was a home where the cow had to be milked, chickens fed, water pumped and hauled from a well, and food prepared on a wood-burning stove.

Now, she was again looking at a *wood-burning stove.* A sink and cabinets lined the north wall and *an old fashioned, honest to God icebox* squatted in the corner.

Dad shrugged weakly.

"We don't have any running water," he said weakly.

The Garrett Grimace got deeper.

"Yet. But don't worry. I can rig up a shower, and the toilet flushes.

"Kim goes out every morning with two 10-gallon cans to meet the water truck. And we'll get a block of ice for the icebox every day.

"Kim will take care of everything."

The legendary Grimace could get no tighter, so Mom retreated to the living room where she sank, speechless, into one of the overstuffed chairs.

We all followed her, Kim taking his cue from Dad's remark.

He bowed to "Missus Captain, Sah."

Handing her a large package, he said, "Present-o. Well-come."

Temporarily distracted from her impending nervous breakdown, Mom removed the cloth wrapping and revealed what I thought of then and continue to refer to today as "the ugliest vase in the entire universe".

It was about 16 inches high, heavily glazed jade green porcelain, with bas-relief of *tropical huts and palm trees*. To add to the incongruous design, some kind of spikes wound around the top, like on a dog's collar.

And it was heavy as all-get-out.

Mother managed to mumble her thanks for the "present-o," no doubt hoping there would be no more gifts.

I don't remember having dinner in our new quarters; we probably went to the Officers' Mess.

I don't remember my mother pitching an all out fit that night, either.

I do remember, however, crawling wearily into my new bed in my new room with two windows in my new house—er, quarters, still feeling the rocking of the ship beneath me before I fell into a deep, peaceful sleep.

Within the next couple of days, my mother accompanied me to my first day of third grade in Seoul American Dependents School, one of the first to be run by *DODs, (Department of Defense)* which would soon encompass the world. I was relieved to see that the huge dome covered mostly an attached auditorium, which served as a base chapel on Sundays. The classrooms themselves were not any larger than those I had been in Stateside.

This was February 1947, and within the next three months, I finished my third grade class work. I began experiencing some problems with math. Long division had disappeared somewhere between Oklahoma and Korea.

English and geography were a snap, however. Brats could put a map of the world together as easily as a Stateside child could walk to his school; after all, by the ripe old age of nine or ten, most of us had already been halfway around the world.

With the advent of vacation, my family and I explored our new environment. Like many ancient cities, Seoul was walled, and we visited all four gates. At the Kings' Tombs, a magnificent park with huge stone lions marking gravesites, Gary and I couldn't resist hopping on top of the lions, and for once, our parents didn't scold us.

We took a train northward to the 38th Parallel intending to picnic in an out-of-the-way place, where we thought we wouldn't encounter constant crowds of curious natives. Gary promptly fell into an icy stream, and Mom stripped him bare and laid his clothes out to dry beside a cool grotto where we began eating our Spam sandwiches.

In a moment, scores of natives emerged from the rocks and watched every move we made. We were becoming rather accustomed to the Koreans stares; after all, enduring curiosity was a small price to pay for occupying their ancient land.

If I had thought the Korean winter was the worst weather I would ever experience, I was wrong. Summer sizzled.

Unable to sleep, I lay awake on sweat-soaked sheets listening to the ancient bell downtown tolling, "*Ama, Ama.*"

I reviewed the legend I had been told: A bell maker wished to create the purest, clearest sound in the world, but no matter how hard he tried, nothing would do. One day, after praying to the spirits for one last chance, his young daughter, the delight of his life, raced through his workshop, stumbled, and fell headfirst into the molten liquid. Her cries of, "*Ama, Ama*" (*mama, mama*) were the last words she uttered.

It was just a fairy tale, of course. My favorite was Rapunzel, the princess in the tower who longed for her prince, and who let down her hair for him to climb up to her. As an adult, going through a divorce, my counselor surprised me by asking what my favorite fairy tale was.

"Rapunzel," I replied.

She smiled. "Good. Most women choose either Cinderella or Sleeping Beauty. Yours is a good choice for your life. Both Cinderella and Sleeping Beauty were passive, waiting for someone to come rescue her. Rapunzel, on the other hand, took some initiative for herself."

And that's the way I lived my life, and would continue to live my life. I told her I learned that at an early age: I'm a Military Brat.

Sometime during that first summer, our family went on leave to Japan. Now old hands at train travel, we journeyed down the peninsula to Pusan, the southernmost port, where we boarded a small Japanese vessel named "*Shica.*"

Mid-way to Japan, the *Shica* encountered the tail end of a typhoon. Dad happily stood with the captain on the open deck as the ship pitched and rolled while Mom and Gary and I lay in our bunks praying for a quick death.

This would be the *second* time I was grateful to set foot on dry land: the Japanese island of Kyushu.

Our R&R hotel, the Aso Kanko, sat on the rim of an ancient volcano. On the opposite rim of the bowl was a bustling town.

Out of disaster, prosperity rises.

We consulted the small hotel newsletter outlining all the opportunities for adventure, shopping, swimming, or basking in the hot springs.

Our first activity was adventure: a trek up the side of an active volcano.

We boarded a an ancient, rattling bus along with several other passengers.

The bus driver must have been a retired *Kamikaze* pilot,

because he risked death at every hairpin turn. We could see our final resting place hundreds of feet below.

About halfway to the summit, he stopped the bus, and we unwrapped our white fingers from the seat rests.

"Famous sulphur springs," he announced.

The smell was almost overpowering, and I barely took a moment to read the sign that described the fate of two young lovers. Hundreds of years ago, a young man and woman, whose families denied their request to marry, jumped together into the boiling springs.

"Japanese version of Lovers Leap," someone commented as we again boarded the bus, and our suicidal driver resumed his breakneck race to the summit.

He brought the bus to a screeching halt at the end of the road.

"We walk rest of way."

Captain Deathwish cheerfully urged us along as we hiked, panting and puffing. I soon discovered the meaning of "hot-footed" as my shoes filled with burning, sandy ash. The air filled with acrid smoke, which made our labored breathing even more difficult.

But the goal was in sight, and as someone panted, "We can't let the little yellow man think he's won *this* war."

At last, we reached the edge of a real, live volcano; one that was still smoking and belching ash.

I gagged as my mouth filled with the fumes. Smoke billowed upward from an unseen cavern and incredible heat seared my skin.

It crossed my mind that we might be in danger, but I reminded myself that the US Army had, so far, taken care of me and would no doubt have declared this trip off limits if there had been any danger.

After a respectable few moments contemplating the awesome power of this natural wonder, we all retreated, as one, down the hillside to the relative safety of the bus and its maniacal driver.

I wouldn't trade that experience for the world, but I wouldn't do it again.

We next chose a visit to the hot springs bathhouse.

We had been told that entire Japanese families often attended this spa, au naturel. Westerners that we were, we clad ourselves in modest bathing suits and entered the hot, therapeutic water.

Moments later, the doors opened and an entire Japanese family of four, mother and father, girl and boy, entered at the other end of the pool.

I had never seen the naked human body, both sexes, grown and immature alike.

I tried not to gape.

The family members bowed respectfully, and we followed suit.

In our suits.

After her slacked jaw shut, Mother recovered her voice.

"We've been in long enough, now." She motioned us out of the pool. "See, the sign says it's not good to sit in this hot water over ten minutes."

Although we had been there for only about three minutes, and I saw no such sign, this was no time to argue with Mom.

The Oriental family bowed to us once more, and we semi-bowed as we passed, thankful that this time, *they* were in the bubbling waters.

Shopping was next on my mother's list. Making sure we didn't have the same driver as our last trip, she and I rode a bus down to the local market where Mom bought four silk scroll paintings:

Two depicted women in flowing kimonos and elaborate hairdos; a black-and white landscape and a peacock in all its feathered glory.

She also purchased an exquisitely crafted porcelain statue of a serene, kimono-clad young woman gracefully holding a ginger jar on her shoulder.

This delicate 12-inch statue survived countless moves over countless years, but it took only one tiny marble to almost destroy it and create a family legend.

We think it was Gary, who, for some unknown reason (neither he or our younger brother, Bobby, will confess to the nature of the dispute) hurled a marble across the room at Bobby.

He missed.

The statue, in its place of honor on the mantel, teetered but did not fall and smash into a million pieces on the hardwood floor.

However, the doll *had* been *decapitated*.

After my mother finished screaming and crying and confining the suspected murderer Gary to his quarters for life, she pulled herself together, got out the glue and carefully set the woman's head back on her shoulders.

This was pre-Super-Glue days, and the adhesive marks were easily seen. So Mom painted a dainty necklace at her throat, and voila! Problem solved.

I think the lady should have her head glued back on properly, without leaving any marks, but I also believe Mom wants to keep the evidence of the crime in full sight, hoping someday, someone will confess.

The peacock painting also suffered a near loss. When we received orders for Europe, Mother, loath to pack it in our household goods, left it in her Aunt Violet's care, in Wichita Kansas.

Three years later, on our way to Dad's next assignment (Fort Hood, Texas) we paused long enough in Kansas to retrieve the painting.

"But I've redecorated the entire living room and dining area to blend with the peacock's tail feathers," she protested.

Six years later, Aunt Violet relinquished the painting and redecorated her house.

After my father died, Mom gave up the house on the hill and moved closer to town. As I was helping her close the house, I asked her what she intended to do with the furnishings.

"I've called the junk man to come and am having him haul off this old stuff," she said. "I've bought all new furniture, and I am having it delivered to the new house."

I pointed out that the Japanese silk scroll paintings were still on the walls.

"We'd better get these down and store them somewhere...."

"Oh, just leave them there. Those old paintings won't go with my new Southwest decor," she sniffed.

"Mom! They're well over 50 years old—and were old when you bought them. I'll trade with you. You remember my two Native American signed and numbered Jerri Leeds watercolors? They'll go beautifully with your Southwestern décor."

Done.

The two Japanese women in kimonos are the first thing one sees when coming in my front door. The landscape is on the stair landing.

The peacock painting, however, watches over the entry hall in Mom's new house.

Before we left Japan to return to Korea, we were invited to the authentic Japanese home of one of Dad's friends. They had a boy about my age, who delighted in confusing me by sliding the rice-paper walls around, so I lost my way every time I left a room.

We ate at least one meal sitting on the floor, and we quite naturally removed our shoes upon entering and slipped on a pair of tabis for the duration.

To this day, I prefer going barefoot in my house. In winter, I will grudgingly wear thick socks.

And then it was time for our journey back to Korea. By ship. I have mercifully blotted out that voyage in my memory, so I can't tell you for sure whether or not I got seasick, but why should this trip have been any different?

School began again, and I was in the fourth grade.

This was the year the school burned. I woke in the middle of the night to the sounds of shouting and the smell of smoke.

"I think it's the school that's burning," my dad said as he joined me at the kitchen window.

Other kids would have rejoiced. I hoped not, and I was relieved the next morning to discover my classroom and others were intact.

Just the auditorium, which had served as a base chapel, had burned. I saw water-soaked Bibles and hymnals as I passed on my way to class.

My teacher's name was Miss Weed, then Mrs. Marcus. We studied the usual subjects, with the addition of Ancient History. I can see that little red book even now, chock full of stories such as the Greeks, the Roman Empire, and Alexander the Great. I fell in love with him. *Of course, he was an army general.* When it came to the part in his story where he "cried because he had no more worlds to conquer," I cried, too.

I cried a few more times in school that year. A feeling of great sadness would suddenly overwhelm me, I would cry silently, still writing my English assignment, or spelling, and it had absolutely nothing to do with anything. I couldn't explain it.

Word got back to my parents, of course, that I was crying in school. Mom didn't understand; I couldn't explain, and Dad was mortified.

"Did you cry in school again today?" he quizzed me at dinner.

There was no use in lying; he would find out. There were spies everywhere.

I nodded and got a lecture from my God, punctuated with his forefinger stabbing the tablecloth, about how I was *not* to cry in school any more.

So I cried at the dinner table.

Then Mom lost her patience. "Now look what you've done! She's crying in her plate!"

And I was, and I had no further interest in dinner.

"May I be excused?" I blubbered, and of course, I was excused; nobody wanted to have any part of my neurotic behavior.

It was years before it dawned on me that I was already entering puberty—at the ripe, old age of nine, and hormones were running riot. I was to experience my first menstrual period in Junction City, Kansas, when I was in the fifth grade.

Who would have thought?

I fled to the sanctity of my room, where I sought comfort in reading, writing poetry or short stories or playing old records over and over.

I was also building a dollhouse from an old orange crate. Turned on its side, it became a two story, four room house, complete with a white "picket fence" (pipe cleaners bent into shape) and a "swimming pool" (one of Mom's discarded hand mirrors).

I populated the house with a family of four—mother, father, daughter and son—and furnished the rooms with curtains, rugs, and furniture.

The furniture was cardboard, cut and shaped into couches, beds and chairs. The inhabitants and the rest of the furnishings came courtesy of the Sears, Roebuck catalogue.

The Wish Book is what my parents called it.

Long before we made the trek to Korea, the catalogue had become part of our lives. As a youngster, my mother depended on mail order from Chicago to provide her with some degree of fashion in far West Texas. Her mother, my grandmother Garrett, bought material and corsets for her corpulent body, and Grandpa browsed for tools and work boots.

So definitely, when we found ourselves halfway around the world in a strange country, the Morris family depended on *The Wish Book* to bring us some degree of civilization. Just leafing through its pages brought us closer to home.

And now, I had virtually destroyed the Sears, Roebuck Catalogue. *The Wish Book.* I had cut my dollhouse family from the fashion pages and ripped the cloth samples glued to the home furnishing pages to become rugs and curtains.

I don't remember my punishment, if any, for this misdeed. Since our purchases kept arriving from Sears, Roebuck, I assumed no real harm had been done. We had clothes to wear, shoes on our feet, and all was well.

There was one fashion crisis, however.

When Mom had left the States, skirt lengths were short.

Shortly after we landed in Inchon, *the new look* dictated long skirts.

I don't recall what the other women in the compound did about this crisis, but my mother solved the problem by taking scraps of material that closely matched that of her dresses and stitched extra pieces of cloth at the dresses' existing hemline, thus creating an instant compliance with *the new look.*

I experienced somewhat of a fashion crisis myself. I was elected (I modestly state) Queen of the May, and as such, it was my duty to lead the Maypole Dance.

In a white dress.

I had no white dress.

It was too late to order one from the half-ruined *Wish Book.* So my mother humbled herself, and me, by inquiring around the compound of women who had daughters about my age if she could borrow a white dress.

Oh, the shame of it all. Here I was, an Officer's Daughter, and Queen of the May, at that, wearing a *borrowed* dress. I don't remember who we borrowed it from, and it doesn't really matter, but I was miffed that my mother had not had the foresight to equip me with a white dress, should I be named Queen of the May. I was almost as fashion conscious as my mother.

Our household settled into a comfortable routine, except that shortly after we arrived, our quarters caught fire.

Others were to follow, as the fireplaces had been faultily constructed.

On that frigid February morning, I was the one who first noticed that something was wrong.

I was sitting on the floor in front of the fireplace, Dad was reading, I believe Mom was in the kitchen, and Gary was undoubtedly being *numbah one son* with Kim when I saw white puffs of smoke billowing up from the floorboards.

I hesitated to say anything for fear I might be mistaken, and then, Daddy would scold me. I wasn't exactly afraid of my father, but I was afraid of making a fool out of myself in front of him, so I pretended a lot—pretended that I knew something I didn't, that I heard something I didn't hear, and now—now I was seeing something I wasn't really sure was what I was seeing.

But the smoke continued, and I began feeling uneasy.

I'd better say something:

"Daddy. Look. There's something coming out of the floor."

I didn't call it smoke, in case it wasn't really smoke. Dad brought down his paper and looked, then frowned, then leapt from his chair.

"We've got to get out of here, right now!"

He yelled for my mother and Gary and was herding us out the front door.

Getting on the phone, he reported our quarters as being on fire.

The rest is a blur. I don't believe we lost a thing, as the military responded instantly, but that same day, we moved to other quarters.

So what to do for heat? First, GIs and Koreans came bearing what appeared to be a sandbox. On closer examination, it *was* a sandbox, which was plunked down in the center of the living room. Next came a group carrying inside an old-fashioned, black, pot-bellied stove, which they set down in the middle of the sandbox.

Then, they left.

The Garrett Grimace appeared and stayed for days.

The stoves worked well, radiating safe heat in the immediate area, but they certainly played hell with the furniture arrangement.

Some time later, our unfortunate neighbor across the street lost everything when his quarters burned to the ground.

Only the toilet was left standing bravely amidst the ruins.

Aside from that minor interruption, the household routine became as follows:

Morning. We wake to the sounds of the water truck grinding to a halt a couple of doors away. Kim grabs two 10-gallon empty olive drab metal cans and races the other houseboys to his station at the water truck.

The empty cans are quickly traded for two full cans of water.

A brief gossip session with the other houseboys ensues, (one morning, practicing his English in front of the other houseboys, Kim reported that Missus Captain Sah had got up before noon, and he told the others: *"Sun rise in West today; Missus Captain up before noon."*) and then, Kim races back to the kitchen banging the screen door as he enters and deposits his load.

Mom wrote to Grandma Garrett: *The only time we have running water here is when our houseboy picks up the cans and runs with them.*

Mother soon adjusted to living without "modern conveniences," as she realized all the other women were coping with the same situation. And she could teach the "city girls" how to cope

Water procured, poured, shower taken via Dad's primitive rigging, I breakfasted on cereal which came from a rock-hard box that must have languished in Army commissaries for the past fifty years or so before reaching Camp Sobingo, Korea.

Cereal thus pounded into manageable proportions in my bowl, I poured bottled Avocet cream, diluted with water, over the stuff and forced it down.

Never one to like milk, this was an even greater abomination, in my opinion, but I had to eat something, and this was it.

Gary, meanwhile, was in Kim's room, happily eating breakfast (fish heads and rice) with the houseboy.

He then ran into our mother's room and crawled into her bed.

"Ye Gods!" Mom shrieked. "What is that smell?"

"I've been eating Korean chop-chop with Kim," he breathed into her face.

"Well, don't do that any more," she said getting up mostly to escape the smell that permeated the bed sheets.

Gary began to wail.

"But I wanna eat Korean chop-chop with Kim."

"Well, okay," she relented. "But when you do, you can't come get in bed with me. Okay?"

A terrible decision for a three-year old to make.

But he chose his morning chop-chop, and Mom got to sleep a little longer.

Dressed and ready for school, I picked up my schoolbooks and homework and bolted out the back door.

I would never be late for school. This was not allowed.

I passed a bank of tall trees on the left of the lane, hearing the familiar and comforting mourning doves cooing in the early morning light. I loved this part of the day and can remember even now the smells and sounds of those mornings in that far-away land.

On that road to school stood a guardhouse. What the guard was guarding, I have no idea, but that's the Army for you.

Normally, I passed the native guard with just a simple nod of recognition.

One morning around Christmas, he spoke to me: "You Christian?"

I nodded. *(Don't speak to strangers, my mother's voice echoed in my head.)*

He spat.

"Pah! Christians!"

Terrified and mystified at the same time, I ran the rest of the way to school wondering about his remark, and didn't tell anybody of the strange encounter.

That followed my family pattern. Don't tell anybody anything.

Despite the guards' presence, compound residents lost property with amazing regularity:

One of Mom's friends was listening to the radio, going about her day when she suddenly felt something was wrong; she wasn't sure what, exactly, and then, she realized she no longer heard the radio.

Going to the spot where it usually sat on a small table under the screen less living room window, she thought the electricity must be out again.

"Wrong," she said later to her friends at bridge. "The *electricity* wasn't out—the *radio* was! I poked my head out the open window just in time to see a young Korean guy running toward the wall with our radio tucked under his arm.

"Stole it right from under my very *ears*," she laughed.

During our "routine" days, when I was at school, Mom was playing bridge, or at the Officer's Club planning an Officers' Wives function, and Gary was playing around under Kim's feet; Dad went "to work."

It was always a mystery *where* and *what* Dad's "work" was. Nobody talked about it.

Least of all Dad. There was absolutely no such conversation as: *"How was your day at the office?"*

He did appear every evening for dinner, except for the times when he was "on maneuvers"—and that was often.

Maneuvers were necessary as we were to discover a year or so later. Russian troops were just north of the 38th Parallel, that invisible, soon to be infamous, line of demarcation.

Which would not normally cause us any problems in Seoul, but these were not normal times.

The Russians had control of our electrical supply. At any given moment, *"Uncle Joe" (Stalin)* would "pull the plug" and the Americans would be left with no power. Movies ground to a halt, but only temporarily, as generators were quickly pressed into service, and the latest Betty

Grable movie or *The Song of the South* proceeded with only a slight interruption.

Another irritation with the Russians occurred at the movie theatre downtown—a rare treat—as we usually attended the "local" movie "house" on compound.

We were ensconced in the large balcony of the huge theatre, waiting for the start of the movie, when three commanding figures loomed up out of the dark.

I literally felt my father tense at the sight of three Russian officers staring down at us.

"We sit here," one gestured grandly.

Dad nodded his head, the international gesture of good will.

This was evidently not good enough, for the leader repeated, *"We sit. **Here.**"*

Of all the empty seats in the theatre, upstairs and down, they wanted *our* seats!

Dad motioned for us to stand; we moved across the aisle, and the Russians settled themselves in our former seats with great grunts of satisfaction at having bested the "*Amerikanski.*"

I don't remember if we stayed to see the movie, and I don't remember the name of the movie, either.

It doesn't matter, of course. What mattered is that we avoided an *international incident*; a term every Military Brat of that era would come to learn by heart.

The Red Cross sponsored a carnival across from our compound, and I, craving excitement, insisted on attending. Mother had given me some military scrip to buy a few items from the Post Exchange; instead, I hiked across the highway and plunked down my (Mother's) money so I could *"See the Red Bats!"* Red bats, huh? This must be pretty amazing.

I entered the booth, anticipating the find of the century—only to see: Two *baseball bats*, painted red.

I lurched out of the booth and ran home.

My mother's wrath upon discovering that not only had I not been to the Post Exchange for whatever it was she needed, but I had "lost" the money instead, didn't compare to my feelings of shame, disappointment, and anger that I had been duped.

It was years before I could muster enough enthusiasm to attend a carnival, and then it was with a jaundiced eye.

A "Post Exchange gene" must be in our family, because years later, in Austria, Gary, about age eight, "appropriated" some five dollars or so out of Mom's purse, and he hiked to the P.X. annex close to our housing area.

Mother saw him later dragging home a heavy bag, about the same time she discovered she had been "pick-pocketed."

Confronted, Gary nevertheless stood his ground as Mom interrogated him.

"What did you do with the money?"

Gary opened the sack to reveal can after olive drab can of—GI foot powder.

"Ye Gods," she exclaimed. "Why on earth did you buy this?"

"Well, it was on sale," he said proudly. "It was a bargain."

Stifling her laughter, Mom marched him back to the Post Exchange annex to return "the bargain."

Besides movies being interrupted by power outages in our compound in Seoul, homework suffered, too.

But not for long.

"Having no electricity in your quarters is no excuse for not doing your homework," our teachers warned. "You still must do your homework."

They knew every household had been issued one or more Coleman lanterns, and like Abe Lincoln, I did my reading by firelight. And homework was handed in the next day.

We were also the proud owners of an electric iron; Kim took great delight in doing our ironing. What he lacked, however, was patience. When the electricity would suddenly be cut off, he swore eloquently in both English and Korean.

He also lacked a sense of hygiene: scorning the sprinkler bottle that my mother had shown him, he preferred swigging a large mouthful of water, then "spraying" it over the clothes.

Mother raised her eyebrows and repeatedly handed him the sprinkler bottle, yet Kim persisted

Mother finally gave up and looked the other way. There were worse things, she supposed, than wearing clothes that had been "sprinkled by spit."

Our houseboy's full name was Kim Yung Kyu, and he held absolute dominance over household matters. Even mother found she had to tread lightly on such matters as ironing and stoking the wood stove, and any other household routine.

Kim frowned mightily whenever he felt his authority was being challenged.

That was one reason we had great difficulty keeping a house-*girl*.

In our brief span of two years in Seoul, we had three housegirls. They came; they served, and they departed: E Chung Soo, Moon Sung Che, and Mrs. Kim.

Mrs. Kim was *not* our Kim's wife. He let that be known immediately upon her hire.

I believe E Chung Soo was the first house girl. Kim interviewed and hired her himself, as he did subsequent others. Mother had the final say, officially, but in reality, Kim was in charge of the housegirls.

Nobody lived up to his expectations, and he was constantly nagging and berating the girls.

I bragged to my classmates that I could cuss in two languages.

Of course, I had no idea what the words meant in Korean, and not much more what the English words meant, but I knew cuss words when I heard them.

Moon Sung Che came next. Mom had trouble with the multiple names, so she decided she would call her "Suzie."

And Suzie she was, except to Kim, of course. We never found out what infraction she created to get herself fired, but Kim managed to let Suzie go, too.

Mrs. Kim, an older woman, was not easily intimidated by the young man. Peace reigned at last, and Mrs. Kim stayed throughout our remaining tour.

A stray dog wandered into our yard one day and adopted us. Kim suggested we name her "Migi." She disappeared one day only to return carrying puppies in her mouth.

We had no trouble distributing the puppies throughout the compound, and Gary had gained a companion.

I don't recall what happened to Migi, but I suspect that when we left Korea, she transferred her loyalty to Kim.

At the 1999 Overseas Brats Reunion at DFW, during one of the many seminars discussing All Things Brat, someone brought up the subject of leaving our pets behind. We could accept leaving toys, dollhouses and other treasured possessions, and we regretfully accepted their loss. But to part with a living, breathing companion with fur or feathers was heartbreaking, and our grief is felt decades later. Grown men and women, recalling their loyal "Spots" and "Fidos" wept openly, many for the first time since their initial departure.

Winters were brutally cold, and I developed chronic bronchitis. Gary, not to be outdone, came down with chronic tonsillitis. Mom kept the compound doctor busy making house calls where he dispensed foul-tasting pills for my bronchitis and gave Mother the bad news that Gary's tonsils would have to come out as soon as we returned Stateside.

I kept my bronchitis, however, until I was in the 8th grade, when it vanished overnight. I had "outgrown" it, the doctors said.

Good riddance, I thought.

Summers were spent playing softball in the bare yard. If nobody was around, I entertained myself.

Gary also found ways to create a playground out of nothing.

One day he placed one end of a board on the edge of the porch, the other end on the ground, and declared he was going to walk up the plank.

I told him no.

He said yes.

I shrugged.

He walked and slipped, and a rusty nail, sticking out of the board, sliced through his upper lip.

Bloody murder couldn't have been louder. I thought he was dying.

So did our mother.

She whisked him off to the compound dispensary where he was patched up and brought home.

Gary has that scar on his lip to this day, and he never lets me forget it, either.

Radio was also my companion. Armed Forces Radio played music from the recent war years, and I knew them all. If I didn't listen to the radio, I had records, generally of the same genre as the radio, but I didn't care.

And there were parties. Lots of parties.

One in particular was a housewarming that the others in the compound threw for us shortly after our arrival.

Throngs of young men in uniform filled the house, and liquor flowed freely, along with snack foods.

Parties lasted long into the night and sometimes into the next day.

Many of the men were unaccompanied; that is, either they were not married with children, or their wives and families declined to join them for their tour of duty in such a foreign place. These young men were all my "Uncles."

I claimed "Uncle Stretch," "Uncle French," and many others.

Clearly, these young men were lonely and craved a family life of some sort, and they doted on my family.

While I called them "Uncle," they referred to my dad, mother, myself and brother Gary as: "Moe, Miz Moe, Miss Moe and Little Moe."

When answering the telephone (oh, yes, one of our few amenities) in our quarters, besides the requisite, "Captain Morris' quarters, Marilyn speaking," I at times took a chance and greeted callers with "Yovosayo." or words to that effect: "Hello" in Korean, followed by "Miss Moe speaking."

I figured that was okay, since it was friends calling, and probably not the General anyway.

Commissary provisions were mundane, and we soon tired of the same old things.

Canned goods with no labels ceased being a "surprise" meal.

We longed for fresh meat.

So Dad and some of our "Uncles" organized pheasant hunts bringing home myriads of the birds, which Kim painstakingly cleaned and removed all the buckshot—at least all he could find.

We found the rest as we were eating.

We ate baked pheasant, broiled pheasant, fried pheasant, pheasant and rice casserole, etc. until we decided "pheasant was pleasant" but could we just lay off for a while?

What we *really* longed for, we decided, was Mexican food.

Mom wrote to Grandma in Texas, requesting a care package of canned Mexican foods.

The day the Ashley's Tortillas and Enchilada Sauce arrived was a day to celebrate. We felt like we were home again.

Mom invited Mrs. General to lunch. A bold move. But Mrs. General was warm and kind, and not at all pretentious. "I saw her in the commissary this morning," one of Mom's bridge playing friends reported. "And guess what? Her slip was showing!" Hot gossip, indeed. The lady was human, after all.

Mom had cooked such a massive quantity that we had some food left over, and the next day being my ninth birthday, she suggested I bring some classmates home for a Mexican lunch.

We had a feast.

I also had a party at the Officers' Club with all my Uncles in attendance. I have a snapshot of a grinning nine-year old in plaid skirt and white blouse standing in front of the Club; it could have been taken anywhere on earth; it was so typical.

But it wasn't a typical place on earth.

It was primitive, hostile at times, exasperating dealing with constant theft, lack of running water, fresh meat, vegetables and the Russians above the 38th Parallel.

When at last our tour was up, we departed Korea at the opposite end of the peninsula from where we had landed: From Inchon in the north, to Pusan in the south.

It didn't matter, of course. We were going home.

This Pacific crossing on board the *Simon S. Buckner* would be a little easier than the prior journey with fewer seasick days, and when the ship passed under the Golden Gate Bridge, I cried with joy and relief.

The first thing I wanted after we landed was to go to a soda fountain, where I ordered a milkshake.

And I didn't even like milk. But I was determined to have what I hadn't had in all those months.

I followed the milk with a large bowl of ice cream.

I could wait for the fresh meat and vegetables.

After a day or two in San Francisco, we headed down the coast toward Los Angeles in our jeep, which Dad had arranged to bring with us. Her name was "Puddle Jumper" if I recall correctly.

As huge trucks passed us, poor Puddle Jumper shuddered in their wake while I, of course, got carsick.

Carmel, beautiful Carmel by the Sea, seen from my vantage point crammed into the back of the slow-moving vehicle, side flaps whipping in the breeze, was not so impressive.

At the jeep's top speed of 40 mph, it took us a long time to reach LA, where Dad's Uncle Marvin lived. He helped us locate a good car lot where we patted old Puddle Jumper goodbye and traded her for a fairly new Ford, and we continued on our way to Fort Riley, Kansas.

We visited relatives along the way, of course.

At one time in my grown-up life, a friend of mine and I were driving down I35 toward Boerne, Texas, and as we passed through Temple and Austin, I remarked each time, "I have a cousin who lives there . . ."

My friend, being an only child, and not a traveler like me, was amazed.

"You have a lot of cousins in a lot of places," she remarked.

I did. Some I liked more than others. But they were all accommodating to us.

In Junction City, Kansas, we rented a large, two-story house with huge trees in the front, which cast shadows on an already dark and gloomy structure.

Rentals were extremely high, post-war, so it was necessary to share the house with another couple.

The wives shared the kitchen—none too successfully— as both women had her own idea of how a kitchen should be run.

The Chinese character for "trouble" is two women under the same roof.

I had a room in the attic, which both thrilled and scared me. The thrill was that I had a very private place of my own, but the very steep and narrow stairs were scary. I had a fear of some *thing*, or some *one* swooping down on me.

I hurried up those stairs as fast as I could to the safety of my room. Nevertheless, this room was all mine, and I spent hours pretending—ice skating, being a ballerina—after all, I was only nine years old.

The basement of the house in Junction City, Kansas, was sinister, too. The door creaked when it was opened or closed. That was about the time I began listening to *Inner Sanctum* on the radio.

One story told of a dangerous fugitive hiding in somebody's basement, and I shivered in terror anytime I went near the basement door.

I was now in the fifth grade, but my recollections of that school are almost a blank slate. It wasn't terrible; we changed classes, going from one classroom to another as our subjects dictated and that made me feel grown up.

Some of my classmates had never even been out of their own city, so they certainly couldn't relate to me, a well-seasoned traveler at the tender age of ten, being dropped into their small world.

I'm amazed that I can't even remember one classmate.

Maybe it was because I was there for such a short time, because Dad immediately applied for, and got, orders for Europe.

And oh, yes, Gary had his tonsils out while we were there.

Germany sounds like a nice place, I thought.

From Ft. Riley, we drove to New York City, stopping along the way . . . well, you know the rest of the sentence . . .

At some point, we obtained an *air conditioner for the car*—it was a small version of a "swamp cooler"—placed in the driver's side window, air flowed through the tube, over a pad and out the other side—voila! Cooler air.

It worked very well—until we reached the East Coast. Hot, muggy weather greeted us at the entrance to the Holland Tunnel, the same time as a New York cop.

"What dat ting dere?" he asked Dad while we were stuck in a long line of traffic.

"It's a car air conditioner," Dad replied.

"Huh! I seen it all, now," was the only comment from the cop, and we crawled on to our destination: Fort Hamilton, in Brooklyn. We were to wait until we received our port call, which turned out to be for Westover Field, Massachusetts.

These few days have blurred except for a couple of "snapshots" in my mind:

The Hormel All-Girls Band practicing on the polo field and . . .

Our walk through Grand Central Station, an absolutely magnificent, cavernous, all marble building, like a huge museum, to board a train to Massachusetts.

All I know was our plane had four engines.

Dad had taken flight training at Shepard AFB in Wichita Falls TX right before the end of the war, and he was unabashedly excited about the upcoming trans-Atlantic flight.

My mother and I had some reservations, if not trepidations about flying, and I, of course, promptly became air sick, almost before we departed.

I wrote in my diary just before take-off: "On the plane flying to Germany."

We first landed in Newfoundland, where we refueled and took off again. Next came the Azores. We had a slight layover, and upon take-off, there was some kind of engine trouble, and we immediately turned back. I have blotted that incident from memory.

Thanks be to God, we landed for the final time at Rhein-Main Airport in Frankfurt. It was there that the reality of the recent war was impressed on me forever. Debris lay in the streets; buildings were no more than rubble, stacked high, and citizens were scavenging for food, clothing, anything useful.

We may have been the victors, but I did not feel victorious.

At the *Bahnhof*, we boarded a train where our destination at last revealed to us: Hoersching, Austria, was Dad's post; the city was Linz, Austria.

Whatever happened to Germany? I wondered.

The train took us through the Russian Zone, where Russian troops boarded, late at night. I was sleepy and tired, and my parents told me in low tones to cooperate as the guards examined our passports (and faces) before grudgingly allowing us to proceed. I just as grudgingly put on what I hoped was a nonchalant face.

I added that incident to my mental list of annoyances the Russians inflicted on us.

Around midnight, the train halted in Linz, Austria, and we tumbled off the train into the station.

Someone in uniform met us and escorted us to our temporary quarters, apologizing profusely that housing was not quite ready for us.

But we would, he assured us as we clambered wearily out of the jeep, be perfectly comfortable at *The Linzerhof.*

He showed us to two rooms and a bath—but the bath was a common bathroom at the end of a long hallway. I was too tired to care and promptly went to sleep in one of the big featherbeds.

I was awakened the next morning by the sounds of church bells, pealing mightily. After quick visits to the bathroom down the hall, we were ready for breakfast. We were practically the only souls in the spacious dining room and ordering from the menu was tricky, but we managed to get a hearty meal; lunch and dinner were taken in the same room.

Did I mention I had thought we would live in a castle? That bubble burst rather quickly that night as we all came down with raging cases of diarrhea, and, remember, the bathroom was a long way down the hall.

After a week in the hotel, Mother put her foot down. Dad was on the telephone almost hourly to the Housing Officer. Desperate, he offered us a house outside the military housing area, but "suitable for our needs."

"We'll take it," was our chorus, and thus, we bid a fond farewell to *The Linzerhof* and made our way up the hill beside the Danube to *#10 Donatusgasse.*

It was almost a castle, I thought: a huge, three story stone house, with the garage on the lower level, then our living quarters, then living quarters for another family upstairs.

Entry through the garage was by huge winding staircase, onto a large landing, where glass doors opened onto our area; the stairs continued on the other side, to the second story.

Our neighbors on the upper floor were a Colonel Stein and his wife, and we speculated that he was with the CIC, as they were both very quiet and closed-mouthed. We gave their huge German shepherd, Sigone, ("Gypsy") a wide berth at all times.

The doors from the landing opened into the dining area. A pull-down light fixture hung over the large oak table. Gary spent a good deal of time pulling it down and then watching it draw back up towards the ceiling until Mother cured him of that practice.

To the right of the dining area was the kitchen, all white tile and very utilitarian. A bathroom was off to the side, and Mom and Dad's bedroom.

On the other side of the dining room, the living room was furnished with a sectional sofa, quite *avant-garde* at that time, nestled under wrap-around windows.

Since the castle had only two bedrooms, I had to share my room with five-year-old Gary, and the Princess was not pleased. However, we managed to coexist for the year that we lived there.

#10 Donatusgasse --- then and now.

A housemaid and a janitor, or Housemeister came with the house. Herr Lehner lived in the basement. Unable to return to his homeland, he soon immigrated to Canada about the same time that we moved from #10 Donatusgasse to an apartment in Bindermichel. I never knew his first name.

Our maid, Maria, was a large, raw-boned woman from Romania. She sported a gold front tooth and had the most enormous feet of any woman I had ever seen.

Maria's 13-year-old daughter was ill with tuberculosis in a sanatorium somewhere away from Linz. Whenever Maria did the laundry, my clothes "somehow" shrank.

Mother, exasperated at the latest laundry fiasco, said she suspected Maria did it intentionally, hoping my sweaters would shrink to fit her child. But she kept quiet about it, feeling the sick girl needed the clothes worse than I did.

Whatever *Maria Of the Gold Tooth's* faults were, she redeemed herself by baking the most delicious apple strudel we had ever eaten—and have not found duplicated since. I watched, fascinated, as she rolled out the pastry dough, and painted it with egg white. It became so thin that when she held it up, we could see through it.

The smell of baking pastry, filled with sliced apples and spices, permeated the air and lodged deep in my sensory memory.

Ah, Maria's apple strudel.

One of those fond memories of Brat-hood.

We were also fortunate to have fresh bread delivered to our door daily. Still warm, Mom and I hacked at it, smeared the huge chunks with real butter and feasted as soon as it arrived.

One morning, the bread man evidently wanted to talk to "the Frau."

"Vo ist Mama?"

Gary, who had answered the door, called, "Mama?"

Hearing her voice from some distance away, Gary marched to a door, threw it open and announced proudly, "There ist Mama."

On the toilet.

Number 10 Donatusgasse's surroundings were green and lush in the summertime and draped gracefully with snow in the winter. The better part of the front yard was covered with a wide driveway from the gate to the garage, so the "real" yard was at the side: a peach orchard that yielded the most delicious fruit.

Shady in the summertime, fragrant with blossoms in the spring, our side yard became a Mecca for parties my mom and dad seemed to have quite often.

I often gazed out over the Danube from my perch in the Spanish Guard Tower. This site's history was vague, but the local populace was convinced that it had stood there since the early days of the Roman Empire. Nobody was quite sure how it came to be called the "Spanish" Guard Tower.

The tower was a short walk from my house on Donatusgasse. A trail led through a wooded area emerging at the base. I either climbed up the stairs to the top or merely lingered in the garden, looking out over the flowing Danube.

Dreams were born here.

I took delight in acting the part of Rapunzel, letting her hair down from the tower in which she was imprisoned, allowing her Prince Charming to climb up her hair and "rescue" her.

Occasionally, as I gazed out over the Danube into the Russian Zone, it occurred to me that if *I* could see *them*, *they* could see *me*. A chilling thought, which I put out of my mind the instant it intruded.

I was, after all, the daughter of an American Army Officer, and, as such, I felt protected.

Since we were warned *never, ever to cross the bridge into the Russian Zone*, we were thus astounded that it didn't work with the natives.

Gary's bike was stolen. No sooner had we reported it to the local authorities, than it was recovered—across the river—in the Russian Zone.

Evidently the thief depended on the military's restriction about crossing the Danube and felt it safe to ride the bike across the bridge. No matter how it was recovered, Gary was happy to have our MPs return his bicycle.

Summer time was delightful with warm, sunny days and cool nights. I spent a great deal of time in the Tower and in the park nearby. I even scratched my name in a wooden bench; unfortunately, on my return to Austria in 1996, I didn't remember having done that, or I would have sought it out. And perhaps after these many years, the benches must have been replaced,

We took advantage of Dad's liberal 30 day leaves and planned two "tours" of Europe: The first venture was to drive to Innsbruck, then on to Venice, Monte Carlo, up the Grenoble Highway to Paris, and return via Germany.

Our second tour, alas, was cancelled because my mother was pregnant with my brother, Robert Lynn, and was advised not to travel. I still tease him about costing me a trip to Holland, England and Spain.

We set off on the first leg of our adventure in our trusty little Renault with the motor in the back. I can still hear the roar and feel the vibration as the little car gasped its way slowly along the famed Grenoble Highway.

I'm sure Napoleon had a reason for choosing this route from Southern France into Paris, but *he* didn't have to contend with an engine roaring in his ears all the way.

On our way to Innsbruck, we stopped at a Gasthaus for lunch: a huge loaf of bread, a round of cheese of unknown origin, grapes, apples, sausage and wine. I still believe this is the most civilized of mid-day meals.

Arriving in Innsbruck near nightfall, we checked into a hotel, washed off the road dust, and went downstairs to the opulent dining room.

Gary and I were allowed to drink wine or beer at the dinner table, or as in the above picnic, at any meal where alcohol was an option. Because of our early exposure to alcohol, beer and wine, I believe we adopted a healthy regard for "drinking." I still enjoy a glass of wine with dinner, but Gary, being a Mormon, does not drink.

That night in Innsbruck, as I climbed into my huge four-poster bed with the feather pillows and bedding, the cool summer night air blowing gently across the windowsill, will remain as one of my great memories of that time and place.

Innsbruck at our backs, we headed on to Venice.

"No cars allowed in Venice," Dad told us. We had to leave our vehicle in a lot outside the famed city of canals. From then on, we would either walk or take gondolas wherever we wanted to go.

We had already reserved rooms at a hotel alongside the Grand Canal, and we stepped aboard a water taxi, which delivered us to our destination,

Dinner was served in the sidewalk cafe, and we watched the local populace stroll by and the gondolas glide to and from their destinations until darkness fell.

The next morning, Dad rousted a sleepy son and a grumpy daughter for a tour of Venice. Aboard the water taxi once more, we stepped out at a gondola rental where Dad haggled with one of the "drivers."

Finally settling on a price, the gondolier motioned for us to come aboard.

Never a big fan of water or water sports, I mentally added "water touring" to my list of "can do without." Nonetheless, as we passed through many famed areas— The Doge's Palace glittering in the sunlight; the Bridge of Sighs—I found myself absorbed in the beautiful architecture, ending at St. Mark's Square.

Of all the cathedrals I had seen, this was the most awe-inspiring. Gazing up at the massive clock, I was thrilled to see the two bronze figures strike the hour. I thought of the bell in downtown Seoul, how different the sites were from each other, and how the tones of the bells were completely different.

Back into the Renault.

Monaco was our next stop. Breathtaking in its perch on the hillsides, the town of Monte Carlo dispelled any of my former grumpiness.

At twilight, we were served a seven-course dinner on a deck overlooking the fabled harbor, and after dinner, Mom and Dad went to the casino.

Children were not allowed.

My grumpiness quickly returned.

"I always have to baby-sit," I whined, glaring at my kid brother, who glared back.

"Well, you'll just have to," Mom replied.

"There's nothing to do," I stepped up my protest with the eternal lament of pre-teens everywhere.

"I'm sure you can find something to entertain yourself," was the final answer as the King and Queen departed in their evening wear.

I prepared for bed and yelled at Gary to do the same.

Turning the hot water tap, nothing emerged but a groaning, pipes shaking and banging.

Accustomed to the vagaries of European plumbing, I waited a while and then tried again.

Water flowed, but it wasn't *hot* water.

So? There's no hot water. Hmmm

I sang to myself, to the tune of "O Sole Mio"

"There's No Hot Water,

There's Just the Cold,

Can't Get Hot Water,

This Place is Old."

Gary was unimpressed.

I, however, became rather enamored of my song and continued to sing until I tired of it.

I had, indeed, entertained myself.

Farewell, Monte Carlo.

After a grueling trek up the Grenoble Highway, where I once again became carsick, we at last reached Paris.

Mom and Dad went out a couple of evenings there, too, and I began to wonder if I were doomed to be a baby-sitter forever. Fortunately, Gary and I were included in their daytime excursions, one of which was visiting the Eiffel Tower.

Before we ascended the famous site, Dad took one of his family-famous slides. *(Dad was famed in our extended families for showing his slides from all over the world. One cousin, confused about "Who is Uncle Wayne?" was reminded by another cousin: "Oh, you know: He's the one with **the slides**.")*

That particular shot, upon reviewing today, seems somewhat eerie: We are the *only* people around. The area, which is now thronged with tourists, under and on the monument, was devoid of people. Five short years after the end of WWII, tourism had yet to spring back to life.

That day was June 25, 1950.

We ascended the Tower, and my father purchased *The New York Times, Paris Edition.*

And there is the news that staggers us: **North Korea Invades South Korea**.

"We knew it was going to happen," muttered my father. "It was just a matter of time."

And then the chilling realization dawned: We could be trapped in harm's way should war also break out here in Europe.

Dad grabbed the first telephone we could reach and contacted his base in Austria.

Was he to return to base immediately?

I pitied anyone who had to make that decision. We could proceed with our plans but keep in touch with his unit. The Russians were showing no signs of making any movement in Europe.

Yet.

Our fears unspoken, we traveled on to our friends' house in Germany, but my fear did not evaporate until we neared our home in Linz.

We also had friends remaining in Seoul as part of the Military Government. What had happened to them?

A few months later, I learned of their escape from a Brat who had been in Seoul, and then sent to Linz. At the very first sign of incursion into South Korea by the Northern troops, dependents were immediately gathered in Inchon, where ships were provided for the hasty evacuation.

Unfortunately for this particular Brat, the boat rescuing them was a cattle boat.

And shortly after the ship sailed away from port, it began to rain.

She said she had a choice: Stay on deck in the rain, or go below with the cattle stench.

She chose to get wet.

Another trip highlighted the Eagle's Nest, or, as we called it at the time, "Hitler's Tea House."

Perched high in the Bavarian Alps outside Berchtesgarten, its reputation was that of a hide-a-way for Der Fuhrer and, more so, for Eva Braun.

We boarded the military bus for the arduous one-way climb up the mountain.

Our driver was cheerful and fearless steering us around endless hairpin turns clinging to the edge of sheer cliffs. (Was he somehow related to the Kamikaze driver in Japan?)

We arrived at the top, incredibly grateful to still be alive, where we assembled with our fellow passengers for a briefing on the next leg up to the famed structure.

We would enter through the tunnel directly in front of us. It looked fearsomely dark and sinister, lighted only minimally by small bare bulbs hanging at strategic points from the ceiling.

The guide told us Hitler's staff car drove rapidly through this tunnel directly to the elevator at the end. Then, as well as now, I surmised, mere peons walked.

Our footsteps echoed off the stone tunnel walls; unconsciously, I kept to the side, even though it was away from the dim light. Was I expecting Hitler's staff car to roar down the middle?

Soon we arrived at a massive steel door, which our guide opened onto what appeared to be a rather opulent room, with plush red–carpeted floors and seating.

The walls were mirrored, floor to ceiling, and the lighting was brighter in this room. We took our seats on the long banquettes and awaited further instructions from our guide, who entered last.

"The tunnel we've just come through was certainly more brightly lighted, and Hitler's driver made certain this leg of the ride was very quick.

"Here you will notice the mirrored walls, the bright lights, and most of all, the ceiling." We gawked at the motif on the ceiling. It looked like a daytime sky.

"Intentional, to alleviate Hitler's claustrophobia," our guide continued.

Wheels clanked and groaned as the room moved slowly upward through the mountain to the bottom floor of the Eagle's Nest.

We emerged into a kind of hallway where dignitaries would be greeted by aides, and either announced right away or kept cooling their heels, depending on Der Fuhrer's disposition.

Proceeding down a corridor, we reached an enormous room dominated by a huge window overlooking the idyllic Alps.

This was the famed Map Room that we had seen in newsreels, only the glass was missing from the window. It had been blown out during a bomber attack sometime during the war. Once the center of great power and stripped of its huge map table, the room exuded a haunted quality— haunted by ghosts of failure.

Outside the house, we explored the barren grounds and Dad motioned for me to sit on the rock wall surrounding the area, where he snapped a black and white photo.

It seemed at that time, everything was colored gray. Drab and gray. Rocks, ruins, and debris—all this destruction overshadowed the surrounding countryside, like volcanic ash.

Some forty-five years later, I sat on the same ledge, with my daughter taking a color snapshot. We also posed at the entrance to the former Tea House; the sign behind us tells everyone this is "Khelstein Haus." The German people have erased all traces of any former connections to Adolph Hitler.

When we returned to the United States from our trip in 1996, my daughter and I placed the old and new photographs side-by-side. The landscape now sparkled with colors. The once drab Tea House was now brightly painted, the sky a sparkling blue. It was difficult to believe this was the same site I had visited so long ago.

Before school started that year, I began sleepwalking. I woke several mornings, fully dressed, across my bed, with dew on the soles of my shoes. I had no idea what I had been doing, nor where I had been: probably waiting on the corner for the school bus.

But it was very disconcerting to my mother, and she were relieved when school actually began, and I ceased sleepwalking.

It was the fall of 1950. I caught the school bus at the end of the lane riding with other Brats down the hill toward Landstrasse.

School was my one constant, my lifeline to normal life. There I was with kids from other places, but we were all joined by that common denominator: our fathers were in the military, and our lot in life was to accompany him wherever he went.

While waiting for the school bus each morning, I encountered some of our neighbors, all of them friendly to the American presence. One elderly gentleman passed daily tipping his hat and saying, "Gruss Gott." This expression, loosely translated, as I understand it, means "God Be With You," or "Greetings from God." Bestowed as a greeting or a farewell, the phrase is used only in Bavaria and Austria.

Upon my return to Europe with my daughter, I felt I was missing something the entire time we were in Germany, but I didn't know what it was.

Until we reached Bavaria, and the expression "Gruss Gott" reached my ears. *That's it!* I thought to myself. *It's only in this part of Europe!*

It was a wonderful start to my day then, and today it gives me great comfort, upon entering or leaving my house, to touch the "Gruss Gott" plaque I have nailed to the inside of my front door.

I began the sixth grade at Linz Dependents School, technically, Diestweg Schule for Knaben und Madchen. Our 6th grade class was fifteen to twenty students, at the most, who came and went with great regularity.

In Korea, the principal of our school had been Colonel Leavitt. His daughter, Nan, was in my 3rd and 4th grade classes. None of us girls liked Nan Leavitt, partly because of her father's job—and we were practically honor-bound to dislike her just for that—but also because Nan wore *pigtails.*

Nobody wears pigtails, we sniffed in disdain, and we snubbed her daily.

Flash forward: I'm in Linz, a couple of years later, and sure enough, we find out that we're getting a new principal.

And it's Colonel Leavitt.

And here's Nan, *with her pigtails*, standing in front of the class.

Linz Dependent School

And I welcome her, literally, with open arms. After all, despite her parentage and her pigtails, she was a part of where I had been. She was a Military Brat.

After classes, I took the school bus home, along with the other kids, dropped off at the bus stop on the corner, and trudged homeward.

Same as any Stateside kid. Only the language was different around me.

I even belonged to an honest-to-goodness Girl Scout troop. As we would have done in the States, we wore official Girl Scout uniforms, worked toward merit badges, and we recited the Girl Scout Oath at every meeting.

And occasionally, we took a hike up the hill from the Danube to the Guard Tower, and the courtyard, where there was a friendly Biergarten.

I could imagine the Girl Scout Headquarters' shock if they had seen all eight of us, clad in our official Girl Scout uniforms, quaffing large steins of dark beer.

At some time in the summer between my seventh and eighth grades, our classes went on a field trip to stay the weekend at Bluhnbach, near Salzburg. It had once been a Hapsburg Royal Family Hunting Lodge. We went again during winter break the next year.

On the summer trip, we clambered aboard a horse-drawn sled, which pulled us up and up, into the mountains. The Hunting Lodge had now become a Rest Hotel for military and dependents, and we were the lucky visitors this weekend. We had it all to ourselves.

The Hapsburg family had ruled the Austro-Hungarian Empire for centuries, and part of the royal heritage, if you will, was to build their residences as if they were medieval castles.

The main living areas consisted of a Great Hall decorated with all kinds of stuffed trophies: Pheasant, grouse, and deer—all of these glassy-eyed animals stared down at us. A music room, complete with grand piano, which we abused terribly with our fervent renditions of *Heart and Soul* and *Chopsticks*. A dining room with a long mahogany table, set with elegant china and crystal; we were seated in massive carved wooden chairs that took all our strength to pull out and up to the table. There was also a game room, complete with pool table; the boys immediately claimed possession.

Accessed from the great hall was a staircase unlike any other I had ever seen. The steps were extremely shallow, and the steps curved, around and around, up and up. I found it difficult to climb these stairs. I likened them to a Fun House stairway, where the steps move beneath your feet, or collapse altogether. I have often thought of those stairs, and that particular stairwell, and my wonderment at how they were built.

I walked in the soft drizzle that blanketed the countryside like a light fog. As I strolled across a wooden footbridge over a small stream, I wondered what persons had passed here before me and what were their thoughts and dreams?

I was utterly comfortable in this foreign land feeling I belonged here. And I knew that one day I would return; if not to this place exactly, then to the country where I experienced my first sense of freedom and autonomy.

At night, after a sumptuous dinner and an hour or two spent in the music and game rooms, we retired to our bedchambers.

Massive featherbeds greeted us. There were two girls to each room, but we could have accommodated many more. We couldn't resist bouncing on the bed, opening the window to admit the cool night air, and then burrowing deep inside the eiderdown.

Ah, bliss. Bluhnbach, Austria in the summertime.

The next winter, our class returned to enjoy the opportunity to ski—that is, *others* were given the opportunity to ski. For some reason, even though she signed the permission slip to go to Bluhnbach, my mother did not want me to ski, and I pouted a lot about that.

In retrospect, I realize my mother and several others were wary of their kids being injured in a foreign country. Even though we had adequate medical care through our military, it would have been particularly frightening to have a child injured and treated on foreign soil, perhaps without the latest and greatest medical equipment and knowledge.

We were pulled up the mountain by an honest-to-goodness horse-drawn sleigh, complete with "bells on bobtail." Huddled together on the frigid ascent, we arrived at the mansion and gathered gratefully around the roaring fire in the ornate fireplace.

That evening, the massive featherbeds were a particular joy.

Since I couldn't participate in skiing, I passed my time with a few other "non-skiers" in the game room, or in the music room, or simply contented myself with reading in the great hall trying to ignore the stares of the stuffed animals on the walls.

How fortunate I was, I thought. Even at that age, I knew I was experiencing more than even some privileged, wealthy kids could ever hope to attain.

But I'll bet *their* mothers would have signed their permission slips, so *they* could ski, I sighed.

Summertime was when I felt free to roam the downtown streets of Linz. After school, instead of boarding the o.d.military bus, I turned instead to the "O" bus (the local bus system) and rode downtown.

By myself.

Strolling in and out of the shops on Landstrasse, I generally paused at a pastry shop for *Linzertort* and *café mit schlag*.

Then, I headed for home, but not before climbing up to the Tower overlooking the Danube for a few moments dreaming.

My mother certainly did not worry about me. I certainly didn't worry about me, either.

In the winter, Gary, at his tender age of six years, dragged his sled up the nearby hill, yelled *"Aus der Bahn!"* (out of the way!) and happily careened downhill. He arrived home before dark grinning from ear to ear with his mittens frozen to his hands.

The Seventh and Eighth grade classes were in one room. Miss Sophie Schreiber was our teacher.

The first day of class, she asked us each to write an essay. Accustomed to dashing something off quickly and being praised for haphazard work, I finished before anyone else and sauntered up to her desk where I deposited my paper.

I had barely settled back in my seat when Miss Schreiber summoned me up to her desk.

"You can do better work than this," she admonished quietly.

My cheeks blazed with embarrassment.

I was, as they say, "busted."

Of course, she was right. I could do better, and I should have. Partly angry and partly chagrined, I returned to my seat where I re-wrote the essay.

I learned a valuable lesson that day: No matter if your work had been considered superior in one class, or school, it would be different here. Here, I was expected to do my very best.

Miss Schreiber told my parents that she thought I could skip the seventh grade, but they decided to keep me with my class. I would have been even more out of place in another school besides being "the new kid," if I were younger than the others, too.

That year, we moved to Bindermichel. A quadrangle of housing about four or five stories high, apartments all, I suspect Bindermichel was like a little Brooklyn.

Neighbors knew their neighbors; kids played kickball in the courtyard; we rode our bicycles to the PX nearby. The school bus stopped and collected us all in one spot, and we grew to know each other there.

All of us were not "squeaky-clean" kids, as it happened. Two of the neighborhood boys took a notion one night to set a fire.

Under a jeep.

The explosion was heard for miles.

And all the kids were lectured, of course, about the dangers awaiting us if we didn't behave. I don't know what happened to the perpetrators. It was all pretty well smoothed over and quickly forgotten.

Our apartment was probably pretty much like the rest: Upon entering a small hallway, straight ahead was the kitchen, where *Maria of the Gold Tooth* reigned supreme.

Off to the side of the kitchen was a small room, which Dad, an avid ham radio operator, appropriated as his radio shack.

Wherever we went, Dad installed his radio shack. I can still hear the sounds of static from such far-away places as Australia, England and yes, even the United States. We spent many nights talking to my Grandma Morris in the States via ham radio. Dad contacted a ham operator in her area; they agreed upon a time where she could be at that person's house, and Dad would call.

The only problem was, *our* time was always in the middle of the night. A good time for her, but not for me.

Off the living room was my bedroom, which was surprisingly large, then a connecting door to my parents' bedroom.

There was also an outside door from my parents' room into the hallway, but this was rarely used.

I got the mumps that year. Rotten timing. It was during Christmas break; the whole two weeks, I was confined to quarters. Mom put Gary in my room day after day, hoping he would get the mumps, too, but it didn't "take" for him.

I returned to school after Christmas break thoroughly miserable because I had missed some of the most exciting social events of the year.

Some of the teen activities were held in the Prielmeyerhof, the hotel where the high school kids were lodged during the school week. Their fathers were stationed either in Salzburg or Vienna, and there was no high school in either place, so the kids stayed in the dorm during the school week, and took the train home on Friday nights. On Sunday evenings, they returned to the dorm.

During the first year I was in Linz, the dormitory was on an upper floor of the school itself. The school cafeteria was also in the school that year, but the following year, both the dorm and the cafeteria were set up in the Prielmeyerhof, and at lunchtime, the entire student population was bused there.

A portion of the hotel was set aside as a Teen Club. Teen Club activities were regularly scheduled. Dances were a hit any time; never mind that we didn't have the latest records available, unless someone just arriving from the States had brought some along. That person was very popular, as was any new arrival who had fashion news from the States.

Many nights, the room was a mass of teens swaying to the music in the dim light. It could have been a scene in any Stateside club, except for the mural on the walls: Austrian Alps, "gingerbread" houses and castles stretched the length and width of the room.

Our other hangout was at the Gugelhof, an old mansion fairly close to Donatusgasse. In fact, all things brat were fairly close, and we walked to a good many places. I traversed the hill to Froschberg many nights to visit my friends there. The Gugelhof was the site for proms and was the setting for my 8th grade graduation ceremony.

Movie Night, at the Gugelhof, was a favorite, especially during the summer. We arrived early and sat in straight-backed, gilt chairs rowed up in the great hall anticipating the movie of the week.

One summer night, the offering was *The Thing From Outer Space,* one of the first great science fiction movies ever made. Truly suspenseful, the audience never got a glimpse of "The Thing" that terrorized an arctic military base until the very end, thus raising our anxiety.

For those unfamiliar with the movie, it begins with an object crashing into the ice near a military installation at the Arctic Circle. Bit by bit, we discover the configuration of the crashed object (a flying saucer, of course) and— gasp— there's a . . . a *body* encased in the ice. The expedition loads the block of ice into the plane and brings it back to the base.

And, of course, *The Thing* is accidentally thawed out, and it begins wreaking havoc upon the inhabitants of the military base.

In one scene, the searchers are in the laboratory, where the latest kill has taken place. They notice blood dripping from a wood box, and when they open it, pistols drawn, out drops . . . a dead dog.

Eventually, of course, reason prevails, and the humans conquer the invader and all ends well.

In the movie, that is.

Things had not ended so well for us, however. We had lingered too long after the movie ended giggling in nervous fright, and we missed the last bus to our housing areas.

Uh, oh. What now?

We'll have to walk.

Of course, the distance was not great; we had walked home from the Gugelhof, many times before, but that had been in *daylight*.

Now it was nearing midnight.

And we had just seen *The Thing From Outer Space.*

"We'll have to cut through the park," one of the braver boys suggested. "That's gonna get us home sooner."

We agreed we would all walk together with different ones peeling off the group as we approached different housing areas, until the last one arrived home safely.

We entered the once familiar wooded area, which, in the darkness, was now forbidding and sinister.

Pretending to prepare the way for us to pass safely through the woods, the boys walked ahead of the girls. They paused at one of the wood boxes stationed in the area until we caught up with them.

"Looks just like the wooden box in the movie," someone said. "Wonder what's in it?"

"Open it," a boy challenged. "It might be *The Thing.*"

Brave laughter from the boys.

"Don't," one of the girls whispered. "I'm scared."

Of course, that was just what the boys needed to hear.

The box creaked open, and . . . thud! A large log fell to the ground.

Screaming in fear, we fled through the park, emerging on the other side. We paused in the open street, breathless, our hearts pounding.

"You guys!" one of the girls scolded. "You scared us to death!"

"Shh," one of them cautioned. "Someone might hear you."

"Yeah," another said solemnly, "*The Thing* might hear you."

We hurried along the narrow, cobble-stoned streets; the huge brass doorknockers on either side of the street seemed to thud in unison as we passed.

At last, the first housing area was in sight, and a couple of the girls and a boy peeled off reaching the safety of their quarters.

Then, two more girls split off. And at each area, there were fewer of us left to fight *The Thing*.

At last, we reached Froschberg. Waving goodnight to my companions, I scurried into the house, safe.

The other kids were on their own.

Mom and Dad had gone to Garmisch for the weekend, leaving Gary and me with our new maid, Katie, who was only 17 years old.

Katie normally did not stay overnight but returned each evening to the Displaced Persons Camp where she lived with her grandmother and little brother. Tonight, she would be in the upstairs bedroom, but *lots of protection she'd be*, I muttered as I ran up the stairs to my room and hurriedly undressed for bed.

Now came a dilemma: Should I close the bedroom door so *The Thing* would have to crash through it to get me, or should I leave it open, so I can see *The Thing* coming up the stairs?

I decided on the former, closed the door, jumped into bed and pulled the covers over my head.

Now every time *The Thing From Outer Space* is shown on television, I relive that long ago night in Linz, Austria.

When I met Joyce Griffith Markins before

Homecoming '99, I asked her if she remembered that night. We were, after all, in the same class at the same time, but she answered that she didn't remember and probably wasn't even there, because she lived in the dorm. Even at the tender age of fourteen, she missed out on the activities of us townies. I'm sure she has memories of being a "dormie," too, but I wished I had someone else who could share the memory of that night with me.

A natural sense of exploring our surroundings led my mother and me up the steps, past the Steins apartment, and into the huge attic of #10 Donatusgasse.

When I remember our foray into that attic, the hair on the back of my neck stands up as it did that day so long ago.

My mother and I surveyed the treasure trove: Nazi memorabilia, helmets, and swastikas on everything. Which, being women on a mission, we overlooked in favor of a stack of material in the corner.

Pleased with ourselves, we dragged the bolts of material from the attic. Iridescent taffeta became my prom dress. Black lace became an overlay for my mother's pink, silk, New

Year's gown.

Before we retreated from the attic, I discovered an unusual silver coin, with a picture of a bishop or a pope on one side, and a design on the other. I couldn't fathom its significance, but I did note that the coin had stamped on it: 1688.

A few years ago, I determined the coin was probably commemorating the opening of the Mirabel Gardens in Salzburg, at which Bishop Albertus presided. So if it was a commemorative coin, and not dating from 1688, perhaps it was issued in, say, 1938, and thus, not really valuable. But who knows? At some point I might have the wherewithal to have it appraised by a rare coin dealer, or something.

Until then, it's just a memento of my foray into an attic in Linz Austria in 1950.

Dances in the Teen Club were highly structured. First was a Grand March led by our teachers. Then, came the regular dances for which we used dance cards. Between dances, I chatted with the high school students, hoping my boyfriend, Tom Wynne, would sign my dance card. And he usually did.

Tom was a year ahead of me in school, and thus, a "man of the world," in my eyes. He came to my house in Froschberg (he lived in that area, too), and we sat on the couch holding hands while my little brother Gary hid behind the couch and snickered every few minutes.

When we departed Linz via train, Tom rode with me as far as Wels where his parents picked him up. He held my hand the entire way and gave me a box of chocolates and a handkerchief as parting gifts.

Nice boy, that Tom.

Dad's promotion to Major called for another party in that house. Mom and the other women were in a dilemma because a Negro officer was invited, there would be dancing, and—gasp—what would they do if he asked her to *dance?*

You'll have to remember the climate of the times— 1950s, before Civil Rights, before there were such terms as Black or African-American. Back then, a person of color was a Negro.

The *Negro* officer provided the obvious solution, of course.

He did not ask *any* of the women to dance.

My fourteenth birthday party was also held on the terrace and in the backyard. Catered by the Officers' Club, we had a large sheet cake, sandwiches, soft drinks and snacks, and the party was a huge success.

One reason it was successful, I believe, was that guests at both parties felt free to wander through the French doors to the terrace, then back again to the refreshment table, thus ensuring a nice flow of conversation and mix of personalities. I resolved then and there to someday have a house with French doors and a terrace.

The Gugelhof also had French doors leading onto a huge terrace with stone steps leading down into a beautiful garden. At my 8th grade prom, couples made sure that they wandered out into the garden at least once to steal a kiss or two without being caught by our chaperones. No wonder I like French doors!

It was while we were living in Froschberg that Dad brought home a cute little German Shepherd pup, whom we named *Ginger*. His constant companion, she lived upstairs in Dad's radio shack. A smart little pup, we agreed; she housetrained quickly and was a good watchdog.

One day, however, she became sick, and began convulsing. Despite the vet's best efforts, distemper claimed her life.

I had never seen my dad cry before. As he picked her up and placed her in a footlocker for burial, we all cried with him.

Ginger's remains are somewhere in the countryside around Linz, Austria.

A note of irony: My "baby" brother, Robert, born in Austria, recently acquired a German Shepherd. As far as the rest of us know, he never knew about Dad's dog, so it was particularly startling when, upon wondering what to name her, he let his youngest daughter decide. "Ginger," she said, emphatically.

Our classes made field trips to further our education. One I was not particularly enamored of was a visit to the iron and steel works in Linz. Just beginning its recovery after the war, Linz was struggling to regain its principal designation as an industrial town. We wandered through the guided tour of the huge facility enduring the heat from the blast furnaces as workers poured molten metal into forms.

Another field trip was into the countryside where we walked along paths while our teacher challenged us to identify the various types of vegetation. I was not particularly interested in this activity, either, and to this day cannot tell an oak from an elm tree.

What really fascinated me was our trip to a monastery. I gravitated toward its ornate decorations, music and sense of reverence. While the other kids shivered and made sounds of disgust, the trip down into the catacombs, walls lined with skulls of former inhabitants, didn't bother me. I wanted to examine each skull, wondering who this person had been, and what kind of life he had led.

The site of a recently excavated Roman bathhouse also got my attention. Just think how ancient this bath was! It didn't look like much at the time, but I could imagine how ornate it had been in its prime.

It was around this time that one of my favorite radio programs on The Blue Danube Network aired the *You Are There* series, providing me, the listener, with a first hand account of the destruction of Pompeii in 79 AD. When I became a freshman at Fort Hood High School a couple of years later, my research paper was—of course—the destruction of Pompeii.

Not all of my school days were academic and not all full of parties and dances.

There was a factor that hung over our heads daily, which we attempted to ignore, and, for the most part, succeeded.

That factor was, the too-near presence of the Russians.

While the threat of war was real and ever-present, I somehow felt protected. Placing my faith in my father, the US Army, my country, and my God, I knew we dependents would be taken care of. We would escape before any invading force.

Therefore, I was surprised when my second husband literally shook with fear as we crossed the borders of Canada and Mexico.

Armed with his passport, he was utterly miserable the entire time we were in a "foreign country." He did everything but continually look over his shoulder, into dark alleys, for an enemy to suddenly launch a strike.

"We could be caught in a war and held prisoner," he defended vigorously.

"Oh, for heaven's sakes," I sputtered. "We are in no danger. The last time I checked, the (Canadians, if we were in Canada, or Mexicans, if we were South of the Border) are friendly nations. Besides, we're American citizens."

But he didn't quit sweating until we returned to our home soil.

Same husband and I, driving west to Abilene, TX over a long, boring stretch of highway. Husband raised his hand, pointing, "Look over yonder at that tank."

I looked "yonder."

I saw no tank.

I told him I didn't see one.

"Yes, it's over there." He pointed again.

144

"Oh, you mean a *stock pond.* I was looking for a *Sherman tank* to come lumbering over the hill. You know, like they used in the war."

Sigh. I should have known right then that our *mixed marriage* wouldn't last.

Military brat and civilian kid will never understand each other.

Military Brats, however, understand one another. We seem to have certain radar to find each other. Don't ask me how it still works as grown-ups. I never did understood it when I was an active Military Brat.

It just is.

Someone once posted as a joke on our Military Brats newsgroup, a test that would determine whether one was a "real" Military Brat or an impostor. (Some trolls so envy us our kinship that they try to fake their way into our online newsgroup. They never succeed.)

I had a problem with the idea, however, for several reasons.

First, as a female, I did not know names of various pieces of warfare, equipment, or supplies.

Second, as an **Army Brat**, I was unfamiliar with Air Force lingo or any other branch of service's acronyms.

Third, as one of the older generation, (stripped of my epaulets, if you would, in 1958,) I missed out on such things as GI dog tags these dependents wore while overseas during the Cold War. That was after my time.

On the other hand, as one of the first dependents sent to Korea, I did know about the hardships of no running water, no fresh fruits, etc.—whereas those Brats "serving" in the

1970's in Germany had no idea what we "pioneers" endured.

But we are more alike than we are different.

We all missed our fathers when they were sent either to war or to another station unaccompanied.

We grieved for our friends' fathers, who went away and never came back from such wars.

And when we received orders to go to another post, we undertook the dreaded, but necessary, task of "unhooking" with our current friends and classmates.

Sometimes our friends departed first. They were in class one day and gone the next. There were empty chairs. In a few days, however, those empty seats were filled with new arrivals, and the process began all over again.

"We'll never see each other again," was our unspoken lament. So Long, Farewell, Auf Wiedersehn, Adieu. See ya. *Not.*

Our focus then became settling into our new schools, our new environments, and finding new friends. Rarely did we have time to focus on our most recent loss.

Looking ahead, never back. Looking back was too painful. Looking ahead to the unknown but boundless future, was full of promise and adventure, and maybe next time, *we* would not *have to leave* or *be the one left behind*.

My departure from Linz was one of the most gut-wrenching events I've ever had to endure.

This was where I had spent my most formative years. This was where I had met my first love.

This was where I found my own life, my independence, *myself.*

When the time came, Dad drove our vehicle slowly down the wide concourse lining our quarters in Froschberg, Mom in the front with my baby brother Robert, born in Austria, Gary and I in the back seat.

I couldn't help but look in the rear-view mirror, at our home, our neighborhood.

Tears began to well up and the dam burst. Sobbing, sniffling, gulping large hunks of air, I *wailed,* an unseemly thing for a young lady of my station in life.

Mother, attempting to comfort me as best she could, managed to blurt, "Don't cry. You'll make new friends."

I could tell she was near tears, also, choking her words out.

I wanted to say, "But I don't want new friends. I want these friends."

Of course, I knew that was impossible and my mother was correct. I *would* find new friends in the new place.

After Tom Wynne unclasped my hand and left the train in Wels, I was to continue on to Leghorn, Italy, with my

family, to board yet another ship, bound for the United States.

Like all good Brats, I knew I had to go.

But I didn't have to like it.

And I didn't. Although it was a very nice ship, and I got a roommate who had been studying art in Italy, I still wanted to remain behind.

And evidently, my roommate did, too, because she immediately began to weep, and when I asked her what was wrong, she just shook her head and cried even more.

Well, at least I had somebody to cry with.

And even though I was on our voyage home, I was once again struck by that half-panicked, half-excited feeling that always assaulted me whenever we got orders. *What would the next place be like?*

As our ship approached Gibraltar, I stood on the deck marveling at that huge panorama before me, Morocco on one side of the ship, Spain on the other. I once again felt that subtle, almost comforting shift from fear towards the excitement level.

But I didn't have too much time to enjoy that feeling; as soon as we passed from the blue Mediterranean to the green Atlantic, I also turned green.

Seasickness descended on me.

I thought if I heard The Bell Sisters crooning *Down in Bermuda* one more time, I wouldn't make the effort to toss my latest meal overboard; I'd just deposit it right there, on the deck.

As we neared The Statue of Liberty, tears of pride and joy filled my eyes just as they had years earlier, when our ship had passed under the Golden Gate Bridge.

Setting foot on dry land—my own country's dry land—I encountered another phenomenon: *Culture shock.*

Culture shock is generally thought of in the reverse: You enter a foreign country and find it very strange and unsettling for quite a while. I did experience it to a certain degree. But I certainly didn't expect it to happen when I returned to my own country!

I had lived in a foreign land for three years, hearing and reading foreign words around me. I soon adjusted and this language became commonplace.

Now, however, all the *foreign* words were gone, replaced by the *English* language. All the advertisements were in *English*. Every billboard, radio commercial, the cab driver who took us to Fort Hamilton—everything was in English.

Commercials were foreign to me. Advertising for a certain brand of cigarettes? How long had they been doing *that*? Billboards depicted scantily clad women urging everyone to purchase a certain make and model car. Where are the *Renaults*? The *Morris Minors*?

By the time we headed down the Eastern Seaboard, and while I was still intensely interested in reading every billboard possible, I had discovered the wonder of television, and my attention switched to that new marvel.

We would not be close enough to a relative's house by nightfall, so we began the family ritual of finding a decent tourist court. This time, however, I do believe we would have willingly occupied roach-infested quarters as long as the sign outside boasted, *Television.*

Mother and Dad agreed on one rather quickly, I thought, and we settled into one large room with *a television.* It operated like a washing machine in a laundermat: Dad provided an ashtray full of quarters to feed the hungry appliance. We hovered in the darkness, wordlessly focusing on *Playhouse 90* until the quarter ran out, and the screen abruptly went black.

We were about to discover who the murderer was!

"Quick! Another quarter!"

A quarter was inserted, the mystery solved, and then, there came another program where, in the midst of the puzzle being resolved, the television abruptly went black . . .

Another quarter, another program . . .

We must have stayed up half the night, plugging coins, until we agreed we didn't necessarily have to finish the latest program.

When we arrived in Fort Hood, Texas, one of the first things we bought was a television set. It was a Hoffman, with a round screen and everything on-screen took on a yellowish hue.

Dad put the antenna on the roof, attached it to a large pole outside the back door, which ran a wire into the television. There was no such thing as a remote control, only a huge knob with numbers on it. When you wanted to change channels, you turned the big knob, and then, you had to run outside and turn the pole, too, so the antenna would point either to Austin or San Antonio.

Sometimes it worked; sometimes it didn't.

I've already discussed my dislike of Killeen High School and how I was treated. I had found only a couple of other Brats for friends there before transferring to Fort Hood High School. I wasn't enrolled long enough to make any lasting friendships there, either.

So when Dad got orders for Fort Sill, Oklahoma, I was once again apprehensive.

I should not have been, this time.

I was one of the more fortunate Military Brats who got to spend all three years of high school with one class through graduation.

That was due in large part because Mom and Dad made another sacrifice for me. After the Korean War, Dad had been ordered back to Korea as an Advisor to the ROK. Mom, Gary, Bob, and I were in another rented house, and rather than have the landlord demand his house back on a whim, my parents bought the house. My next three years of school were assured.

On one of my first days of school, I fell in with about six other girls, not a one of them a Military Brat. I was accepted as though I had lived there all my life, attended the same church, and ran with the same crowd. Why and how these civilian kids accepted me in their midst is still a mystery (although one of them insists, "But you were different.")

We now affectionately refer to ourselves as *The 50s Girls* and for them, I feel truly blessed.

Today, I have the good fortune to have found others of "my kind" through the Internet. The first thing I did once I got connected to the wonderful World Wide Web was type in the words "Military" and "Brats." Up popped the *Military Brats Registry*, and I registered. Almost instantly, I found some twenty former students of Linz Dependent Schools, none of them former classmates, but high school students. But I didn't care. They had been in the same place at the same time as I, and the thrill of discovery has never left me.

However, even before I plunged into the Internet, plain, old-fashioned detective work led me to my first find.

As with most things, it was strictly serendipity.

While reading the morning paper one Saturday, sipping coffee and generally getting my day started, I glanced through the Letters to the Editor, and the words "Overseas" and "Brats" caught my eye. The letter was promoting a regional get-together of *"Overseas Brats,"* an organization *whose purpose is to reunite Military Brats with those former classmates they thought they would never see again.* The writer's phone number was listed, and I wasted no time in calling for details regarding the meeting.

I also wondered where this group had been for the last few years, and why I hadn't known about it before.

But better late than never.

About 25 of us met at a restaurant, where I mingled, for the first time in many years, with people who had experienced the Military Brat life, and I felt at home again. At this meeting, I also received information regarding an upcoming workshop to be held in Dallas by *Overseas Brats* President, Joe Condrill.

I couldn't wait to get there.

My "civilian" friends, however, were puzzled.

"Let me get this straight," one said. "You're driving to Dallas, by yourself, when you hate the Dallas traffic, to a meeting where you won't know a soul?"

"But you don't understand," I explained. "I do know them. They're Military Brats."

I don't think they understand, even today. But that doesn't matter.

I went and took careful notes about how to locate lost classmates and friends. Among articles on display at the back of the meeting room was a list of those who had participated in the Washington D.C. gathering a year or so before.

Categorized by countries where these dependents were stationed, I searched for "Austria" and although I found no listing for Linz, I did see one registrant who had lived in Vienna, at approximately the same time I was attending school in Linz.

The way the Military Brat life worked, even if we hadn't known each other then, we most likely had friends in common. So I copied his name and address, went home and wrote a letter, asking him if he might know the whereabouts of any of our former students in Austria.

Col. Paul Winkel responded, not by mail, but by telephone.

Of course, he knew where some of our "Linzers" were:

"A few of them have been meeting regularly for the last few years. As a matter of fact, the Linz Alumni are going to meet in New Braunfels, Texas, in November. Paul Peterson's in charge; here's his address and phone number."

Thanking him profusely, I immediately called Paul Peterson in Virginia. Explaining that I was merely an 8th grader in Linz, could I come to the reunion?

Of course I could. And he said he would send me a contact list noting that Roxanne Henrich (who was merely a photograph in one of my yearbooks) was living in Dallas, and I might want to get with her to plan our trip to the reunion. He gave me her phone number, and I called her.

She would be delighted to meet me, she said, and we arranged a meeting in the lobby of the Anatole. (By now, I was getting to know Dallas pretty well!) With the passage of years, we knew neither of us would look anything like our yearbook pictures, so I told her to look for "a short, dark-haired woman with a tote bag full of old yearbooks."

And she found me. We hugged like old friends and laid plans to drive to New Braunfels.

At the reunion, at which I felt not at all like a "gate crasher," I was referred to (fondly, I think!) as "the kid." At the Wurst Fest, we drank copious amounts of dark beer. We sang; we danced the chicken dance—it was a little slice of heaven.

Enter the computer. Although I had enjoyed receiving the quarterly newsletter from *Overseas Brats*, I realized the Internet would provide a bonanza for finding fellow Brats. Looking through the Military Brats Registry, I sent an email to those listed as being Linz alumni. Warren Griffith responded to my email, telling me his younger sister, Joyce, had been in my 8th grade class, and gave me her phone number as she was not yet online.

Even though the 8th grade graduating class consisted of only eight people, six girls and two boys, Joyce and I were puzzled that we didn't remember each other.

Then, Joyce said she had arrived in Austria just before the end of the 8th grade, so she didn't have her picture in the yearbook. And, she had been a "dormie," her parents were in Salzburg, and she had to ride the train to and from school each Sunday and Friday.

This was a few months before the August Homecoming '99 at DFW. Joking that either one of us could be an axe murderer, I nevertheless invited her to drive in from her home in Longview, Texas, and stay with me for the Homecoming.

The Thursday before the Homecoming, I arrived home from work to find Joyce waiting.

With her she had brought an enlarged black and white snapshot of our 8th grade graduation: Six girls in white dresses, holding red rose bouquets; the two boys on either side, dressed in their best suits.

Poring over yearbooks, yellowed editions of the school newspaper, *The Scratch Pad*, we relived those bright and beautiful days.

The three-day Homecoming '99 event was exciting, exhilarating and exhausting.

AUTHOR, 5TH FROM LEFT

I had joined an online newsgroup, *alt.culture Military-Brats*, and formed friendships that transcended branch of service, duty station, and age. Now, many of us were meeting face-to-face, and it was as if we had known each other at each duty station and all our lives.

On the other hand, some of our former classmates do not wish to be found. Perhaps their experiences as children of the military were not positive ones, instead filled with violent, drunken fathers, or absentee mothers. Perhaps they didn't make friends easily as other kids, and now they don't want to bring up a painful past.

As the carryout boy at a local grocery store noticed my *Overseas Brats* bumper sticker, he said, "Oh, you went to school overseas?"

"Sounds like you did, too, I said. "Where were you stationed?"

His face darkened, and he practically slammed my grocery sacks into the trunk.

"Okinawa. And I hated the God dammed place."

No interest here, I thought sadly. There are too many like him, I believe, who will not have fond memories of either overseas assignments or of attending civilian schools in the United States. Many of their issues are addressed in Mary Edwards Wertsch's book, *Military Brats: Legacies of Childhood from Inside the Fortress.*

At this writing, *Military Brats Registry International*, founded in 1997 by Marc Curtis when he was looking for his own lost classmates, has over 58,000 Brats registered.

On July 20-23, 2001, I attended the site dedication for the *American Overseas Schools Historical Society Museum.* This historical park will establish facilities to collect, record, display and preserve the rich history (memorabilia, artifacts, records and data) of former students and educators who were deployed as part of the Occupation Forces after WWII.

Until the park is constructed, many of the *sacred relics* from the Brats' pasts are being stored in several footlockers, which travel around the country where reunions are held. The footlockers contain such varied items as: dog-tags issued to dependents, a teddy bear carried by one Brat to each and every duty station, and yearbooks and report cards from various Dependents schools.

Personal contributions include my original report cards from Seoul American School 1947 (4th grade), Linz

Dependents School Linz, Austria 1952 (8th grade), and my very own "orders" issued by The War Department.

As I reflect on those artifacts and all they represent, emotions flow.

This was my way of life, and I knew no other. For the most part, my life as a Military Brat was awesome in that I was given opportunities few others my age could have experienced: living in foreign countries, learning different customs and languages, absorbing and living history every day, so that some day, I could relate to my children tales that began, "When I lived in Korea in 1947 . . ."

Part of my brat legacy has been unresolved grief.

Grief began the moment Dad came home with orders to a new duty station.

On August 21, 1996, RM Morris, Major, US Army, received orders from the Ultimate Supreme Commander

As I sat at my father's bedside, spoon-feeding him Blue Bell ice cream, I already felt the familiar wrenching pain of separation. The little eight-year old girl inside me, who had somehow blamed her father for his frequent absences, suddenly realized that Daddy had nothing to do with his "abandoning me."

He was a US Army officer; he received orders, and he departed.

I had no control over his orders, any more than he had.

Now, he was preparing to leave me again.

During his last few hours, Dad repeated over and over, "I've got to go."

Bless Mom's heart, she kept grabbing the urinal until I said, "That's not what he means, Mom. He's leaving."

I took his bony, yet surprisingly strong hand and told him, "It's okay, Dad. I give you permission. You can go."

All journeys begin, some never end.

ADDENDUM:

I would be remiss if I did not include the following tributes to our Military Brat Mothers, who for the most part, have gone largely unrecognized and unpraised, even among those children they have hauled around the world, from post to duty station, from US to foreign shores, tolerating the nomadic lifestyle while struggling to maintain a "normal" lifestyle for their children.

During a discussion on the alt.culture.Military-Brats newsgroup, it was noted that as we were losing our WWII era fathers at the rate of over 1,000 per day; our mothers were also failing, losing ground, and one of our own Cyber Brats would soon be facing the loss of her indomitable mother, affectionately referred to by all as "Mrs. Colonel."

The original posting brought about an outpouring of sympathy and praises for our own Military Brats Mothers.

The author of the first tribute, Terry Pulliam Hansen, has granted permission to be quoted here, in whole. I felt compelled to respond and indeed, at Terry's request, passed on our comments to my mother, who, in true Military Brat Mother tradition, expressed surprise to receive such praise, and responded modestly, "It was expected of me."

Tributes to our Military Brat Moms

By: Terry Pulliam Hansen

Quoted with permission.

My own mother died nearly two years ago, and I think I'm going to suffer as much with Miz M's passing as I did with my own. And not just because of my love and affection for my Brat pal—but because the last of this generation of mothers is going, and we'll never be able to call 'em back. And we never really "heard" their stories, and we never really respected their sacrifices, AFAICS. These women were WWII brides—they had no idea, most of 'em, what they were getting into, but they smiled gamely for the camera in their catch-as-catch-can wedding ceremonies and kissed their husbands goodbye. And when the men came back, the brides gathered these strangers back into their arms and soldiered on . . .

They were then introduced to the Officers' Wives Manual. (I'm making apologies here, because I don't know what the equivalent EM manual was, but I'm betting there was one and it wasn't any different from the OWs) and were told they couldn't hold a job, because their husband's career was their job. They had to learn etiquette with a capital "E", and Rank with a capital "R." She never, ever, sat Mrs. General next to Mrs. Lt., for instance, and she poured tea from a silver service with short gloves before 6 p.m. and long gloves after. And she volunteered at the base hospital, and she gave birth when her husband was on maneuvers in Greenland, and she held it together when her daughter had pneumonia and he was TDY in Spain, and she soldiered on. And she moved every two or three or four years and she cradled the broken china from her grandmother and tried to piece it back together. And she tried to find a place for the damned camel saddle her husband brought back from North Africa and the Grundig from Germany. And she had no identity that wasn't encased in the plastic Dependent's ID Card—who she was was who he was. And she soldiered on. And she took the abuse her children heaped upon her, telling her how destructive a Military Brat's life can be—how a Brat's life is fraught with pain, separation, dislocation and isolation. She looked into her child's eyes and said, "Yes, I know." And we did not hear what she said.

Okay, you guys, I give up. I can't put a "the end" to this. I would very, very much like to see a chain tacked onto this of the Brats who know what I'm talking about. And then, I want you to give them to your mothers.

Love,
Terry Pulliam HansenTerry "Squeaks" HansenAAC/
AFBV66.0748.CO

Following is my reply:

Tee: What a beautiful tribute to our moms. My mom was what you described, a WWII Vintage, hauling kids from one end of the earth to the other, birthing children overseas, in dusty, remote duty stations, jungles and frozen tundra. Enduring seasickness, inoculations for God knows how many exotic diseases, keeping our shot records, school records, silk kimonos, pets, bicycles, treasured toys (despite household goods weight restrictions - some of her stuff had to be left behind; it wasn't nearly as important as her kids' stuff). Taking us, unescorted, into the foreign countryside, determined we absorb the foreign culture as fully as we could; enforcing "the rules" in Dad's frequent absences, with almost as firm a hand as his, but seasoned with just a pinch of understanding what we were going through. Ordering from the Sears, Roebuck catalog and sweating the exquisite timing for a special outfit for an important occasion, such as graduation from 6th grade, being chosen May Queen, or playing the part of the Princess in the school play, and when the parcel didn't arrive in time, sacrificing one of her very own "ball gowns." A West Texas farm girl training a houseboy and house girl in the Orient one year, in Pidgin English, no less; doing her own housecleaning and laundry the next, and handling both with amazing aplomb. The next year, she begins all over again, training in garbled German-

Austrian dialect with voluminous hand gestures, a giant woman refugee from Yugoslavia as maid, cook and baby sitter, in quarters appropriated from Nazi sympathizers, while keeping in mind that packed suitcases under the beds and Russians across the Danube meant evacuation could be implemented at any moment. Keeping her own grief in check while her kids cry over leaving yet another batch of friends, knowing she might never see her own circle of friends again. Packing, unpacking, making a home with "make do, and do without." Keeping in touch with family back in the Zone of the Interior by letter, written at times by dim lantern light when the Russians in their Zone of Occupation decided to deprive us of electricity at any given time. Myriads more sacrifices made on our behalf. Ordinary women in extraordinary circumstances. God bless "Mrs. Colonel" and her family, and all the Military Wives, from the daughter of "Mrs. Major."

Well done, Ladies.
Marilyn ABV56-042138-01 TX

(The "Code" below our signatures is adapted from suggestions by our newsgroup participants to help identify ourselves: I am AB—Army Brat—V56—Vintage (year graduated from high school) 1956, Date of Birth 4/21/38. Because Joyce Griffith Markins and I share the same birth date, and since I posted before she discovered the newsgroup, I was designated with the "01" after my DOB.. Lastly, since Brats have no place to call "home," only our current location is posted (TX).

APPENDIX:

Contributed by fellow Military Brats

You know you are a Military Brat if you ...

...actually like the clothes at the BX and don't mind that 100 other people are wearing the same thing....all your former very best friends are as long gone as your last move....always wish you were back at the last place you were stationed even 20 years later....answer the question "where are you from" with "I'm kinda from all over the place."...are able to imitate others' speech patterns easily. ...are amazed at people who have lived somewhere more than three years....are amazed at people who have never left their hometown....are amazed at people who have never seen foreign currency....are amazed at people who think Frankfurt is some kind of hotdog....are asked "where did you learn to speak English so well."...are asked "is it hard always moving around" when you don't know anything different....are brought to tears by military music. ...are going to a grocery store but call it a commissary. ...are initially confused when asked where you are from, but quickly respond "everywhere."...ask what they mean when someone asks where you are from....at 22 you are trying to find someone in the military to marry so you can get a new ID card....avoid visiting the doctor because you don't trust civilian hospitals....bagged groceries at the commissary on payday....bought US savings stamps....can ask for a beer in most European languages....can bounce a quarter off your bed sheets and have hospital corners on your bed. ...can call up actual memories of a country while you're in geography class....can identify ranks and duty station by the stickers on the car's bumper....cannot speak the language of the country in which you were born....can recite all of the AFRTS commercials along with the television....can remember ordering a Big Mac, fries, and a beer....can still convert foreign currency in your head....can talk to anyone and everyone from anywhere and everywhere....can't convince a Stateside cousin that your Japanese kimono doll REALLY came from Japan....can't drink Budweiser without being coerced....conceal your father's rank because once people find out he has stars they'll never treat you the same....craved to have a class six ration card. ...didn't save things so you wouldn't go over the weight allowance of the next move....didn't see a TV till you were almost a teenager. ...do not understand why many of your friends are afraid to be in an airplane....don't believe it when someone tells you they never left their hometown....don't feel quite right seeing military personnel younger than you....don't really know how to answer the question "what is your home town."...don't remember the names of your childhood friends....draw a quick map of the world to show someone where you last lived....enjoy seeing guys in fatigues on city streets....ever got sick eating chocolate field rations. ...every room you've ever had was stark white and you couldn't put nail holes in the walls....everyone complains about your name being the most scratched out in their address book....everywhere you go, you think you see someone you went to school with....expect someone else to do your housework but can't afford it. ...feared turning 21 because they would take your ID card away. ...feel like you should be visiting the States rather than living in them....feel more at home on a military base than in town even though you've been a civilian for 26 years. ...feel more comfortable living near a military base and get bummed-out when a base gets closed....felt like a part of history that was happening around you....find that you can easily amuse yourself for hours at airports, train or bus stations....find yourself with friends throughout the world....get frustrated when others talk about going to their hometown to see old friends, teachers, etc....get nostalgic when seeing O.D. Green. ...get the itch to move every 3-4 years and forever feel like the outsider in the civilian world....give someone a break because they are in the military....go into culture shock upon returning to the States....got beer from the Lemonade man at the kiosk....got dressed up and played pranks at Fasching....got grounded or restricted to quarters or put on KP duty....got in trouble on the train to Berlin for taking a picture....graduated from a high school you only attended for a year. ...had a dad who bought you a used SAM to play with....had a father who was always telling you to "police the area." ...had a pup tent in your yard until your parents found out what was going on in there....had a supply of K-Rations that you traded with your friends....had Thanksgiving and

Christmas dinners in a mess hall...had your introductory speech prepared and memorized for your first day at a new school. ...had your school lunches planned and served by people wearing sergeant or private stripes. ...have a collection of beer caps....have a very best lifelong friend whom you have known for less than a few years....have been asked just where in NY APO is....have been hit on at the young age of 13 by men in uniform....have driven four hours to Munich for the taste of a poorly done Big Mac. ...have to explain that being born in Germany does not make you German....have to explain why your ssn is from an APO and your home of record and state of residence don't match....have forgotten how to speak more languages than most people ever learn....have USAA as your insurance company....haven't seen your best friend since the last time Dad was transferred....hear the sound of freedom when military aircraft fly by while civilians complain about the noise....know exactly how horrible AFN commercials are....inexplicably have the urge to move to a new place every year for no reason at all....keep bumping into people all over the world who know friends that you haven't seen in years....kept evac-backpacks by the front door with clothing and passports in case "IT" happened....knew the rank and name of the kid next door's father before meeting the kid next door....know how great it is to be able to return to base and your little slice of America....know how to pack a footlocker....know kilometers better than miles and Celsius better than Fahrenheit....know that Radio Luxemburg was the number one way to keep up with the latest rock and roll hits. ...know the words and tune to military march songs....know what "the land of the big PX" is...know what a jump tower is and after a few beers - thought it made good sense to climb one....know what Ami geh heim or knittle in die buxe means. ...know what the "land of the round door knobs" is...know what the relative value of a pfenning, won, or yen is, compared to the U.S. Dollar....knowing about a variety of cultures....left school frequently for bomb scares....like institutional-style cooking and enjoyed going to the Mess Hall....liked going shopping with mom for an hour and a half drive because the BIG PX sold Canoe. ...listened to Armed Forces and VOA radio for the 1st 10 years of your life....made better grades in geography because you'd been to the places you were studying. ...meet another Military Brat sometime somewhere and are instantly bonded....miss shopping at AAFES or the PX. ...most of your Scout camping equipment had US instead of BSA stamped on it....most of your siblings were born in various foreign lands....munched hot brotchen & gummies on the way to school....name schools in three countries on two continents when asked what high school you attended....never quite finished decorating your place because you knew you'd be moving soon....notice Tom Cruise in uniform, outside with no hat and having a non-regulation haircut in Top Gun....painted a picture on the Berlin Wall before it fell....panic when you can't find your i.d or passport....played American Football at the schwim bad to impress the German girls....polished your father's boots and brass for his upcoming inspection....put your hand over your heart at 5 p.m. knowing the flag was coming down... somewhere....realize that the latest fashion in the States is not the same clothes you bought on base....refer to being in the U.S. as "in the world"....remember following your favorite film as it made the rounds on the AAFES theater circuit....remember being able to watch the Super Bowl or World Series live on TV at 2 am....remember Chris Noel's dedication show on Armed Forces radio during the Vietnam war....remember hanging out at the AYA....remember the Sat. afternoon tank rides at Ft. Hood....say "think opsec" to your friend so they will keep it secure then realize it won't make sense to them....start a major portion of your conversations with "when I was in"......stand up and sing the national anthem at the start of movies. ......still do yard detail!...still get the urge to pack up and move about every 22 months....still look for your ID card after you've grown up....stopped saying "I used to live in Japan" because people kept asking you if you spoke Chinese....talk to someone with an accent and pick it up yourself. ...tell everyone you are from a town that you haven't lived in since you were 4 years old....the oldest friend you have is from your senior year of high school....the term "combat loaded" refers to how the movers load the van. ...think locals have such a limited perspective. ...think of your childhood neighbors' Fathers and Mothers by their rank....think the US seems like a foreign country. ...think you see old classmates on every corner, whether you are in Brussels, Bangkok, or Boise....thought all doctors issued all-purpose capsules for every ache and pain....thought all pens had "US Government" printed on them....thought aspirin came in

5,000 count bottles....thought everyone slept under green or blue wool blankets that had "US" on them....thought that a firing range made a great playground....thought that the Quartermaster was the real Santa Claus....thought vacations meant going Stateside to visit the grandparents. ...told civilian friends Stateside where you lived and they complimented your English....try to remember to drive on the right side of the road....try to take out your ID card when you enter a grocery store. ...use words like "hit the deck," "visit the head" and "pogey bait."...used the federal warnings on your ID card to convince your cousins that you were a military agent. ...waited every Saturday at noon for the alert sirens to go off. ...went in to hysterics when your grandparents thought of selling their house....went out and found everybody leaving on Maneuvers. ...went to school in a converted POW camp....were born in an US occupied country and moved every 3 years....were more interested in your new friend's father's rank than what color your friend was....were pleased to find upon returning Stateside that the locals spoke American....when after 20 years as a secretary you still think of yourself as a yeoman....when battleship gray makes you feel warm and fuzzy....when you can shine your military kid's brass better then he can....when you come to the US and turn on the T.V. and notice that the shows are in English....when you first login to this www site and get the goose bumps....when you see a homeless person and somehow feel spiritually related...when your civilian boss has to ask you more than once not to say "Yes, sir" and "No, sir"....woke up to F-4's zooming overhead. ...wonder if dad signed a hand receipt when you were born....wondered who your new best friend would be as you enroll in yet another school....you make things up about where you are from to avoid the headaches of telling the whole long story....you are confused when your fiancé talks about watching trees grow large in front of the house....you can recite which aircraft were in service in which era....you graduate from 12th grade and it's your 13th school. ...you had your own punch card at the local Class VI store since you were 16...you have climbed down to Survival Beach and back up....you use Scrip or MPCs instead of green backs....you went on weeklong field trips to England, France and Italy....you'd been to every Gasthaus in Germany, both East and West before you were 18....your ssn, home of record, state of residence, and place of birth are far from matching....know transfer meant pack your toys and say see ya later....were in your late teens before you realized flashlight batteries came in any color but OD. you and your friends played army in an abandoned concentration camp.